Readers Respond

"*Get Unstuck*, authored by Bukky Agboola, skillfully intertwines well-illustrated personal stories with epic Biblical heroes, meeting readers at their current point in their journey. It offers more than just encouragement for a brighter future; it provides certainty about what lies ahead for those who trust in the Lord, emphasizing that nothing is beyond redemption.

With practical tools for implementation, *Get Unstuck* equips readers to face any challenges. The author knows the Scriptures well and connects Biblical accounts with contemporary life, ensuring relevance in today's world.

If you're burdened by guilt over past events beyond your control or regretting current circumstances you wish to leave behind, prepare for a transformative experience with the book *Get Unstuck*."

—Steph Carse, 6-time Emmy winner FrontGate Media Team. Platinum recording artist.

"AMAZING JOB. What?! Bukky has done it again! Addressing almost every possible emotion and circumstance that causes us to give up, this book is going to help you understand not just how to keep going but why you need to keep going. I received such clear guidance and so will you. After reading this book, you never have to be stuck again!"

—Ellie M, USA

"Bukky is a beautiful storyteller who also weaves in Bible verses to further illustrate her point."

—Mary H., USA

"So inspiring and filled with truth!"

—Timothy D., USA

"You have a way of fleshing it out in inspiring yet practical ways by looking at the lives of many biblical characters."

—Melanie T., USA

"Bukky is wise, witty, and engaging!"

—Regina C., USA

"The author finds strength in the scriptures."

—Timi O., Nigeria

Get Unstuck

Unleashing Momentum:
The Powerful Key to Your Success!

Bukky Agboola

CHORDS OF LOVE LLC

Copyright © 2024 by Bukky Agboola
Published 2024 by Chords of Love, LLC. All rights reserved.
No part of this book may be reproduced, stored, or transmitted by any means—whether auditory, graphic, mechanical, or electronic—without written permission of the publisher, except in the case of brief excerpts used in critical articles and reviews.

For more information, contact bukky@bukkymusic.com.
To learn more about the author, visit https://bukkymusic.com.

ISBN: 978-1-7335652-7-1 (Paperback)
ISBN: 978-1-7335652-8-8 (Ebook/epub)

Scripture quotations marked NLT are taken from the *Holy Bible, New Living Translation*, © 1996, 2004, 2015 by Tyndale House Foundation. Used by permission of Tyndale House Publishers, Inc., Carol Stream, Illinois 60188. All rights reserved. Scripture quotations marked NIV are taken from the *Holy Bible, New International Version*, © 1973, 1978, 1984, 2011 by Biblica, Inc. Used by permission of Zondervan. All rights reserved worldwide. Used by permission. Scripture quotations marked NASB are taken from the *New American Standard Bible*, © 1960, 1962, 1963, 1968, 1971, 1972, 1973, 1975, 1977, 1995 by the Lockman Foundation. Used by permission. All rights reserved. Scripture quotations marked ISV are taken from *The Holy Bible: International Standard Version*, Release 2.1, © 1996–2012 by the ISV Foundation. All rights reserved internationally. Scripture quotations marked BSB are taken from the *Berean Study Bible*, © 2016, 2018 by Bible Hub and Berean. Used by Permission. All rights reserved. Scripture quotations marked ESV are taken from the *Holy Bible, English Standard Version*, © 2001 by Crossway, a publishing ministry of Good News Publishers. Used by permission. All rights reserved. Scripture quotations marked ESV are taken from *The Holy Bible, English Standard Version*, © 2001 by Crossway, a publishing ministry of Good News Publishers. Used by permission. All rights reserved. Scripture quotations marked AMP are taken from the *Amplified Bible*, © 2015 by the Lockman Foundation. Used by permission. *Contemporary English Version*, © 1995 American Bible Society. All rights reserved. *Good News Translation*® (Today's English Version, Second Edition), © 1992 American Bible Society. All rights reserved. *King James 2000*. Scripture quotations marked TPT are from *The Passion Translation*®, © 2017, 2018, 2020 by Passion & Fire Ministries, Inc. Used by permission. All rights reserved.

Book design by DesignforBooks.com

Printed in the United States of America.

Contents

Chapter One
The Key to Nonstop Progress   1

Chapter Two
He Who Laughs Last   11

Chapter Three
What Gems Might You Discover?   21

Chapter Four
The Process   33

Chapter Five
Don't Stop Pedaling   37

Chapter Six
Use These Key Ingredients   45

Chapter Seven
Don't Stay Disheartened   59

Chapter Eight
Infinite Grace Overcomes Ugly Consequences   81

Chapter Nine
More Is Caught than Taught   101

Chapter Ten
Wait, What? King David Fails Again?   127

Chapter Eleven
How Do I Say This? Yep, It's David Again!   139

Chapter Twelve
Find Fresh Strength in God   151

Chapter Thirteen
A Strong Finish from the King of Momentum!   157

Chapter Fourteen
Who Would Ever Have Guessed?   167

Chapter Fifteen
First Connect with God through Prayers   181

Chapter Sixteen
Then Party   193

Chapter Seventeen
Feeling like the Olives in the Press?   203

Chapter Eighteen
Ask, Seek, and Knock   213

Chapter Nineteen
Move On   223

Chapter Twenty
Refuse to Stay Stuck   233

Chapter Twenty-One
Have a Snack and Take a Nap   237

Chapter Twenty-Two
Reigniting Momentum after a Major Stalemate   247

Chapter Twenty-Three
How to Defeat Haters   259

Chapter Twenty-Four
God's Powerful Example   271

Chapter Twenty-Five
Ruth: The Queen of Momentum   281

Chapter One

The Key to Nonstop Progress

No one can pilot a parked airplane or navigate a parked car. The key to nonstop progress in your life is to never stop moving things forward in whatever positive ways that you can. The Merriam-Webster dictionary defines *momentum* as "*strength or force gained by motion or by a series of events.*"

In other words, by keeping things moving, you will build up the strength to propel your life forward. It is also good to bear in our minds that it's hard for anyone to successfully hit a moving target. While some grave matters will require extremely careful consideration, whenever you're faced with any challenge it is still of vital importance to try to keep things moving forward as much as you possibly can. Don't allow yourself to get or stay stuck. This will make it harder for your opponents to successfully hit, overpower, or overtake you. It makes it more difficult for them to prepare for whatever you might do next. This is a great strategy for staying ahead. Because to be stuck simply means to become unable to proceed—unable to make any progress.

Just imagine a car deeply stuck in the mud on a country road. This can happen to anyone. Because no matter how prepared or cautious we are, no one can always accurately predict what the future will hold. People might unexpectedly find themselves in murky situations. But when we finally free ourselves and gain traction, we're advised to keep moving until we're back on solid ground. This is so that we don't get stuck again or slide back into the mud. This advice is very good to apply whether we get stuck on a muddy road or for life in general. We need to keep our lives moving in the right direction—forward—so that we do not slide back into old negative patterns or get defeated by the same old bad habits.

We just cannot stay in the parked position in our lives if we want to reach our desired destinations.

It's usually not the things in our lives that are going well that tend to make us feel stuck. It's the negative experiences that we may sometimes go through that can induce a sense of hopelessness or despair. But God has promised us in His word—scriptures—that He will grant us the grace to *triumph* over any challenging circumstances or situations. "He said to me, 'My grace is sufficient for you, for my power is made perfect in weakness.' Therefore, I will boast all the more gladly about my weaknesses, so that Christ's power may rest on me" (2 Corinthians 12:9, New International Version). This promise is especially comforting when we're feeling at our lowest or heavily burdened by negative circumstances.

So, if you're feeling low right now, "give all your worries and cares to God, for he cares about you" (1 Peter 5:7, New Living Translation). Because when life has just thrown you a huge curve ball from which you feel like you'll never recover, it becomes even more vital to stay closely connected to God, through His word, and our prayers. "Don't worry about anything; instead, pray about everything. Tell God what you need, and thank him for all he has done" (Philippians 4:6, NLT).

The following verses also tell us what the life of those who draw their strength from God will look like.

> Blessed and greatly favored is the man whose strength is in you. They go from strength to strength [increasing in victorious power] (Psalm 84:5, 7, Amplified Bible; brackets in the original).

> But the path of the righteous is like the light of dawn, which shines brighter and brighter until full day (Proverbs 4:18, English Standard Version).

> And we all, who with unveiled faces contemplate the Lord's glory, are being transformed into his

> image with ever-increasing glory, which comes from the Lord, who is the Spirit (2 Corinthians 3:18, NIV).

Wow! Did you read that? They will *"go from strength to strength, increasing in victorious power," "shine brighter and brighter every day,"* and experience *"ever-increasing glory, which comes from the Lord."*

I'd like to experience all of these in my life, wouldn't you? So, let's all begin to reignite our momentum right now by offering up praises and thanksgiving to God for all that He has already done for us, beginning with our salvation. "Enter his gates with thanksgiving; go into his courts with praise. Give thanks to him and praise his name. For the LORD is good. His unfailing love continues forever, and his faithfulness continues to each generation (Psalm 100:4–5, NLT). When we begin to seek God on a daily basis, we will receive fresh strength from Him to ignite and keep up our momentum at all times, and in all circumstances. He also promises to bless us with His wisdom, guidance, and protection.

> He renews my strength. He guides me along right paths, bringing honor to his name (Psalm 23:3, NLT).

> The LORD says, "I will rescue those who love me. I will protect those who trust in my name" (Psalm 91:14, NLT).

> Whether you turn to the right or to the left, your ears will hear a voice behind you, saying, "This is the way; walk in it" (Isaiah 30:21, NIV).

Our loving heavenly parent also invites all His believing children to boldly come into His presence at any time to seek help. "So let us come boldly to the throne of our gracious God. There we will receive his mercy, and we will find grace to help us when we need it most" (Hebrews 4:16, NLT). Spending time in God's presence deepens our relationship with Him and gives us the grace to live our best lives. Additionally, we're promised rewards for diligently seeking Him.

> And it is impossible to please God without faith. Anyone who wants to come to him must believe that God exists and that he rewards those who sincerely seek him" (Hebrews 11:6, NLT).

> As many as received Him, to them He gave the right to become children of God, to those who believe in His name (John 1:12, NLT).

Having such a loving invitation, and knowing that we're welcomed into God's presence at any time, ought to reenergize us to keep up momentum, regardless of our circumstances. It is our creator who empowers us to become and do all that He has planned for us beforehand.

> For we are God's masterpiece. He has created us anew in Christ Jesus, so we can do the good things he planned for us long ago (Ephesians, 2:10, NLT).

> I can do everything through Christ, who gives me strength (Philippians 4:13, NLT).

We do not have to depend solely on our own strength to ignite or keep up our momentum daily. God's grace is abundantly available to us to refresh and strengthen every area of our lives. The Holy Spirit living on the inside of us helps us to understand His word and apply it to our lives. Start drawing fresh strength from God daily. This is an essential key to your advancement, so that you can begin to make unstoppable progress in all areas of your life.

> And I will ask the Father, and he will give you another advocate to help you and be with you forever—the Spirit of truth. The world cannot accept him, because it neither sees him nor

knows him. But you know him, for he lives with you and will be in you (John 14:16–17, NIV).

I pray that from his glorious, unlimited resources he will empower you with inner strength through his Spirit (Ephesians 3:16, NLT).

And be sure of this: I am with you always, even to the end of the age (Matthew 28:20, NLT).

Despite the humdrum of daily life, begin to unleash this powerful principle of intentionally creating positive momentum in your life to propel you forward. Start right now. We simply cannot remain in the parked position in life and expect to make any progress. Take decisive steps in both big and small ways to get things back into motion wherever you're feeling stuck. Good intentions alone will not move us forward. So, consistently apply this truth to your life. As I mentioned earlier, practicing good spiritual habits on a daily basis, by reconnecting and staying connected to God, is foundational to who we are and all that we do.

Our lives, the amazing planet that we live on, and all the beautiful things that we get to enjoy and have, are gifts to all of us from our loving creator. We may often take this for granted. But God is faithful to human beings even when we do not acknowledge, believe in, or remain faithful to Him. "For in him we live and move and exist . . . we are his offspring" (Acts 17:28, NLT).

> You are worthy, O Lord our God, to receive glory and honor and power. For you created all things, and they exist because you created what you pleased (Revelation 4:11, NLT).

Regardless of any setbacks that you might already have experienced, receive fresh strength from God today to move your life forward. Make creating momentum on a daily basis, starting with your relationship with God, an essential part of your lifestyle. This will keep you from getting or staying stuck. Ignite the release of a continual flow of positive energy and vitality from God into your life that will help you to advance, regardless of your circumstances or environment.

> Yes, I am the vine; you are the branches. Those who remain in me, and I in them, will produce much fruit. For apart from me you can do nothing. You did not choose me, but I chose you and appointed you so that you might go and bear fruit—fruit that will last—and so that whatever you ask in my name the Father will give you (John 15:5, 16, NLT and NIV).

Are you willing to draw fresh strength from God daily to realign and empower you to push past any current difficulties and press on to live your best life?

Chapter Two

HE WHO LAUGHS LAST

You may have heard the popular saying, "He who laughs last, laughs best." But many people are tempted to want to give up or become bitter when their hard work and benefits are stolen by others. For example, you once pitched a brilliant idea to your boss; it gets rejected, but you later watch as your boss pitches that same idea to the higher-ups, and takes the credit for it. He gets promoted and makes no mention that it was originally your idea. Or in another scenario, your valuable invention gets stolen and patented by a much larger company that you had shared your original idea with. Sometimes, it's our closest relatives or trusted advisers who steal our hard-earned wealth or betray us.

It is especially disheartening when people employ foul tactics and still win.

Do any of these examples sound familiar to you? In addition to having our valuable ideas and work stolen, getting repeatedly defeated by the same opponents can leave us feeling completely gutted. If this happens to us, how should we respond? Well, a fine gentleman by the name of Isaac is about to teach us some valuable lessons and show us exactly how to repeatedly unleash momentum to come to our aid. During a conflict over water rights in his community, his enemies repeatedly attacked him. But Isaac refused to give up, put his faith in God, and just kept on moving forward. Amazingly, with this very simple tactic he overpowered his enemies and overtook them, going on to achieve great success.

> Isaac planted crops in that land and the same year reaped a hundredfold, because the Lord blessed him. The man became rich, and his wealth continued to grow until he became very wealthy. He had so many flocks and herds and servants that the Philistines envied him. So, all the wells that his father's servants had dug in the time of his father Abraham, the Philistines *stopped up*, filling them with earth. Then Abimelek said to Isaac, "Move away from us; you have become too powerful for us." So, Isaac moved away from there and encamped in the Valley of Gerar, where he settled (Genesis 26:12–17, NIV; emphasis added).

> Isaac reopened the wells that had been dug in the time of his father Abraham, which the Philistines had stopped up after Abraham died, and he gave them the same names his father had

given them. *Isaac's servants dug in the valley and discovered a well of fresh water there. But the herders of Gerar quarreled with those of Isaac and said, "The water is ours!"* So, he named the well Esek, because they disputed with him. Then they *dug another well, but they quarreled over that one also*; so, he named it Sitnah. *He moved on from there and dug another well,* and no one quarreled over it. He named it Rehoboth, saying, "Now the Lord has given us room and we will flourish in the land." From there he went up to Beersheba. That night the Lord appeared to him and said, "I am the God of your father Abraham. Do not be afraid, for I am with you; I will bless you and will increase the number of your descendants for the sake of my servant Abraham." Isaac built an altar there and called on the name of the Lord. There he pitched his tent, and there his servants dug a well (Genesis 26:18–25, NIV; emphasis added).

Digging a well involves a great deal of work. It's very hard to dig very deeply. It was clearly Isaac's servants who had discovered and dug up these freshwater wells, but they were repeatedly stolen by his envious adversaries. On each occasion, his evil opponents waited until all of the work had been done, and then claimed the well for themselves, giving Isaac and his staff no compensation for all the work that they had done. How infuriated Isaac and his servants must have been. I mean, just imagine the sheer injustice of it all. Surprisingly, this tenacious young man did not waste a single second on any further arguments or fighting with his opponents, but simply reignited his momentum and kept moving. Getting distracted with endless fruitless arguments and battles can be a snare of Satan to get us stuck in bitterness and despair. If he had taken this evil bait, while Isaac was still licking his wounds and feeling cheated, he would have had no water, and his opponents would have been laughing all the way to the wells. Our takeaway?

Do not let any dark forces put a permanent halt to your progress.

Pick yourself back up and receive the grace from God to press on. Let God do your avenging for you. And while you might need a job or department change or take some other actions, be sure to start working on some new ideas and projects right away, as Isaac did.

> Do not say, "I'll pay you back for this wrong!" Wait for the LORD, and he will avenge you" (Proverbs 20:22, NIV).

> Wait patiently for the LORD. Be brave and courageous. Yes, wait patiently for the LORD (Psalm 27:14, NLT).

While your opponents unfairly enjoy the fruits of your labor, and appear to suffer no evil repercussions, trust in God to pay back your enemies just as He has promised. Put more faith in His ability to bless you than in your enemies' ability to hurt you. God has promised to work everything together for your good, and His glory. He will bless you back with much more than you lost. Let all of the injustices that you have suffered become stepping stones, teachable moments to build a far better future for yourself, as this fine gentleman did. This is the best way to prevent yourself from getting ensnared in protracted battles devised by Satan to delay or sabotage you from ever achieving your goals. If you have reached a state of fed-upness and are about to quit, please remember Isaac's story and press on. Because despite the repeated thefts of his wells by the same evil adversaries, he kept plugging his faith into God and moving on as fast as he could. The correct response to adversity is to

Move on and just keep digging!

Dig deeper within yourself to receive fresh strength from the Holy Spirit who lives on the inside of you, and press on.

> And I will ask the Father, and he will give you another Helper, to be with you forever. He is the Holy Spirit, who leads into all truth. The world

> cannot receive him, because it isn't looking for him and doesn't recognize him. But you know him, because he lives with you now and later will be in you (John 14:16–17, ESV, NLT).

This won't at all always be easy. Especially when we've suffered great losses. But I reiterate:

> *Do not let your negative experiences*
> *lead you into permanent defeat.*

Instead, let God help you to overcome them and create fresh *momentum*.

> Brothers and sisters, I do not consider myself yet to have taken hold of it. But one thing I do: Forgetting what is behind and straining toward what is ahead (Philippians 3:13, NIV).

Here is a famous saying by US President John F. Kennedy's father:

> When the going gets tough, the tough get going.

The beloved American actress Lucille Ball also said,

> One of the things I learned the hard way was that it doesn't pay to get discouraged. Keeping

busy and making optimism a way of life can restore your faith in yourself.

The famous British statesman Sir Winston Churchill made the following statement.

> Never give in. Never give in. Never, never, never, never—in nothing, great or small, large or petty—never give in, except to convictions of honor and good sense. Never yield to force. Never yield to the apparently overwhelming might of the enemy.
>
> If we open a quarrel between past and present, we shall find that we have lost the future.

I implore you to start moving things forward with whatever resources that you have left, just as Isaac did. Don't stop until you get to your desired destination. This is a great strategy for recovering from what you have lost and heading toward achieving success. Do not quit on your God-given dreams, especially when you've experienced major failures or defeats along the way. You will have the last laugh if you don't give in. Remember that in order to have the last laugh, you need to keep on laughing. Here is what happened later on between Isaac and his opponents when they realized that he was unstoppable! (Pun intended.) Remember that they kept stopping up his wells?

One day King Abimelech came from Gerar with his adviser, Ahuzzath, and also Phicol, his army commander. "Why have you come here?" Isaac asked. "You obviously hate me, since you kicked me off your land." They replied, *"We can plainly see that the Lord is with you. So, we want to enter into a sworn treaty with you.*

"Let's make a covenant. Swear that you will not harm us, just as we have never troubled you. We have always treated you well, and we sent you away from us in peace. And now look how the Lord has blessed you!" So, Isaac prepared a covenant feast to celebrate the treaty, and they ate and drank together. Early the next morning, they each took a solemn oath not to interfere with each other. Then Isaac sent them home again, and they left him in peace. *That very day Isaac's servants came and told him about a new well they had dug. "We've found water!" they exclaimed. So, Isaac named the well Shibah (which means "oath"). And to this day the town that grew up there is called Beersheba (which means "well of the oath")* (Genesis 26:26–33, NLT; emphasis added).

What a tenacious person Isaac was. He just wouldn't let anyone or anything stop his progress. Instead, he kept things in motion, building up strength as he forcefully advanced in the face of constant opposition. He refused to stay stuck in a conflict with his enemies, which would have wasted much-needed energy and resources that he still needed to dig new wells. Isaac must have thought to himself, "I'll let God avenge me. If He is with me as He was with my father; Abraham, I will surely prevail over them and be blessed." It's a big world out there. There are so many new opportunities. So, let's just keep digging!

> For this reason, I kneel before the Father, from whom every family in heaven and on earth derives its name. I pray that out of his glorious riches he may strengthen you with power through his Spirit in your inner being, so that Christ may dwell in your hearts through faith. And I pray that you, being rooted and established in love, may have *power*, together with all the Lord's holy people, to grasp how wide and long and high and deep is the love of Christ, and to know this love that surpasses knowledge—that you may be filled to the measure of all the fullness of God. Now to him who is able to do immeasurably more than all we ask or imagine, according to his power that is at work within us, to him be glory in the church and in Christ Jesus throughout all generations, for ever and ever! Amen (Ephesians 3:14–21, NIV).

Here is a fun fact: Isaac's name literally means one who laughs! He had the last laugh and laughed best. Creating momentum is a powerful tool for defeating and overtaking our adversaries, and overpowering foul play. He who laughs last indeed laughs best! So, keep laughing.

Do you believe and receive these truths? Will you start acting on them today, starting right now?

Chapter Three

WHAT GEMS MIGHT YOU DISCOVER?

Let's continue to explore this powerful key to success: momentum. There are four brave men from Samaria from whose lives we can learn a great deal more about our theme. Their journey began when they thought that their lives were about to come to an end. While groping in the dark, trying to figure a way out of their horrendous circumstances, they all inadvertently stumbled across this powerful key to success: momentum.

All four men were lepers. As if being lepers in the pre-modern times that they all lived in wasn't bad enough, they'd also found themselves caught up in a long, drawn-out war, when their country went to war against a nation with far superior military forces. Their country was under siege. The war had led to an extreme scarcity of food, and all their nation's citizens faced slow, excruciating deaths by starvation. Both young and old alike were suffering from the terrible effects of severe malnutrition. But conditions were much worse for the poor lepers because, at that time, their disease was incurable. It had almost completely destroyed their health.

These four men, along with all the other lepers in their region, were ostracized from the rest of society. People had a justifiable fear of getting infected with their incurable disease. With their country under siege, they were all in desperate need of a miracle, and at a loss as to what to do to put an end to the terrible crisis. All of their national reserves had been depleted and people's usual sources of income had been blocked by their adversaries. Their enemies had also cut off all the usual avenues through which essential supplies could be brought into their country. People were exhausted from trying to survive in any way that they could, and they all lamented their plight daily. At the beginning of the war, any of the remaining lifesaving provisions in the country would have been heavily guarded. The majority of their country's citizens would not have had any idea where these were. They would have been made available to only the most powerful and influential people in the land. And absolutely no one would have thought that sharing what little provisions that they had left with lepers was a good idea.

The people's life savings were completely gone and, considering the state of emergency that they were all in, there was no time to spare finding a solution to this grave crisis. Lepers were viewed as being of little or no value to the country because of their disease. They could not make any positive contributions to the economy, and the most urgent need at that time was to keep their military forces alive so that they could defend what was left of their country. As hunger ravaged the land, any essential supplies that were left had become more valuable than gold, because there was just nothing to buy. Gold, silver, and everything else of value had all lost their worth. The shelves were empty in all their shops. Going out to search daily for food had become the new national preoccupation.

Despite thinking that all was already lost, people continued to try to overcome their struggles as best as they could. But however much they tried, a slow, painful death by starvation looked certain for all. Everyone scrambled daily to exchange whatever goods, valuables, or services that they had left for food and other essential supplies. Everyone's backs were against the wall, so the four lepers were not at all on anyone's list to receive help. They were all completely drained of strength, and the suffering became more unbearable as the long, awful war dragged on. Their country's previously healthy citizens had also become pale, emaciated versions of their old selves. We can only imagine how much worse the four lepers looked.

When all the nation's supplies finally ran out, some unbearably inhumane behaviors began to happen among the people. Because of their horrific circumstances, they had all lost their natural human compassion for one another. Any hope of making it through the war had long faded from everyone's minds. And any hope of a rescue coming from one of their neighboring countries had also long faded, because no one came through. The only thing left on people's minds was surviving until the next day. The sense of urgency in their once-bustling cities was palpable. The people had lost count of the number of lives that had already been lost. Their country's army was no match for their enemy's powerful forces. Staying alive looked impossible with each passing day, and the four men along with everyone else were all truly stuck.

What should one do if one finds oneself at death's door, and how does one get unstuck from circumstances as dreadful as this?

Amidst all this growing despair, these four lepers are about to show all of us the power that lies in unleashing momentum, because something spectacularly unusual would take place. With seemingly no good options left and hoping to bring a swift end to their misery, just out of sheer desperation, these four men suddenly decided to do something or anything about their plight. Instead of just waiting to die along with everyone else, they all decided to intentionally set things into motion, and ignite momentum, despite their terrible circumstances. The sickness in their bodies and lack of good nutrition for so long had left all of them completely drained of energy. But instead of giving up and surrendering to their grave circumstances, these four brave souls, with barely enough strength left to move around, used all of the strength that they had left to take some *actions*.

We're about to discover how the four lepers, who were so close to collapsing, changed their lives and those of the entire population of their country. I tell you, absolutely no one could have been prepared for what happened next. I hope that their amazing journey helps all of us to commit to reigniting momentum in our own lives and follow through with actions.

> Sometime later, however, King Ben-Hadad of Aram mustered his entire army and besieged Samaria. As a result, there was a great famine in the city. The siege lasted so long that a donkey's head sold for eighty pieces of silver, and a cup of dove's dung sold for five pieces of silver. One day as the king of Israel was walking along the wall of the city, a woman called to him, "Please help me, my lord the king!" He answered, "If the Lord doesn't help you, what can I do? I have neither food from the threshing floor nor wine from the press to give you." But then the king asked, "What is the matter?" She replied, "This woman said to me: 'Come on, let's eat your son today, then we will eat my son tomorrow.' So, we cooked my son and ate him. Then the next day I said to her, 'Kill your son so we can eat him,' but she has hidden her son." When the king heard

this, he tore his clothes in despair (2 Kings 6:24–30, NLT).

Now there were four men with leprosy sitting at the entrance of the city gates. "Why should we sit here waiting to die?" they asked each other. "We will starve if we stay here, but with the famine in the city, we will starve if we go back there. So, we might as well go out and surrender to the Aramean army. If they let us live, so much the better. But if they kill us, we would have died anyway." So, at twilight they set out for the camp of the Arameans. But when they came to the edge of the camp, no one was there! For the Lord had caused the Aramean army to hear the clatter of speeding chariots and the galloping of horses and the sounds of a great army approaching. "The king of Israel has hired the Hittites and Egyptians to attack us!" they cried to one another. So, they panicked and ran into the night, abandoning their tents, horses, donkeys, and everything else, as they fled for their lives. When the men with leprosy arrived at the edge of the camp, they went into one tent after another, eating and drinking wine; and they carried off silver and gold and clothing and hid it. Finally, they said to each other, "This is not right. This is a day of good news, and we aren't sharing it with anyone! If we wait until morning, some calamity will certainly fall upon us. Come on, let's go back and tell the people at the palace." So, they went back to the city and told the gatekeepers what had happened. "We went out to the Aramean camp," they said, "and no one was there! The horses and donkeys were tethered, and the tents were all in order, but there wasn't a single person around!" Then the gatekeepers shouted the news to the people in the palace. The king got out of bed in the middle of the night and told his officers, "I know what has happened. The Arameans know we are starving, so they have left their camp and have hidden in the fields. They are expecting us to leave the city, and then they will take us alive and capture the city." One of his officers replied, "We had better send out scouts to check into this. Let them take five of the remaining horses. If something happens to them, it will be no worse than if they stay here and die with the rest of us."

So, two chariots with horses were prepared, and the king sent scouts to see what had happened to the Aramean army. They went all the way to the Jordan River, following a trail of clothing and equipment that the Arameans had thrown away in their mad rush to escape. The scouts returned and told the king about it. Then the people of Samaria rushed out and plundered the Aramean camp. So, it was true that six quarts of choice flour were sold that day for one piece of silver, and twelve quarts of barley grain were sold for one piece of silver, just as the LORD had promised. The king appointed his officer to control the traffic at the gate, but he was knocked down and trampled to death as the people rushed out. So, everything happened exactly as the man of God had predicted when the king came to his house. The man of God had said to the king, "By this time tomorrow in the markets of Samaria, six quarts of choice flour will cost one piece of silver, and twelve quarts of barley grain will cost one piece of silver" (2 Kings 7:3–16, NLT).

Can you believe what we've just read happened? I mean, matters couldn't have been any worse if women were eating their own children! But these four men chose to set things into motion and headed straight for their enemy's camp, facing whatever dangers might greet them. In what had looked like an absolute dead-end move, these four sick men showed all of us

> *We have no idea what gems we might discover when we simply choose to create momentum.*

So, resolve today to get up and get moving. The circumstances that they were all faced with were far beyond anyone's ability to solve. But whenever we dare to seize the momentum, changes will definitely occur, and this includes the changes that will take place within us. Whether directly at the hand of their enemies or indirectly due to the famine, death had looked certain for all their country's citizens. But by unleashing momentum, they made the most amazing discovery: that God had already gone ahead of them and put their enemies to flight! This proves to us all that

> *No matter how long one has been battling with any negative circumstances, absolutely nothing is too big for God to change or resolve.*

The four men had chosen to disrupt the status quo, when death looked certain for just about everyone. Without realizing it, they had unleashed the powerful principle of momentum to come to their aid. Their entire country ended up receiving a mighty miracle from God, and everyone must have been completely stunned.

> I am the LORD, the God of all the peoples of the world. Is anything too hard for me? (Jeremiah 32:27, NLT).

> Now all glory to God, who is able, through his

> mighty power at work within us, to accomplish infinitely more than we might ask or think (Ephesians 3:20, NLT).

> Ah, Sovereign LORD, you have made the heavens and the earth by your great power and outstretched arm. Nothing is too hard for you (Jeremiah 32:17, NIV).

Overwhelmed with joy, the people trampled over each other to get their hands on whatever they could and wolf it down. Their first reactions must have been disbelief, followed by immense relief. No one could ever have guessed that the end to this terrible famine would have come in such an extraordinary way. Lepers had been considered to be the least likely to have a solution to their nation's direst needs, but they proved to be the ones through whom God would reveal His mighty wonders. The takeaway? Whenever things look completely hopeless to us or we feel powerless to change them for the better, I implore us to intentionally create momentum in our situations, using whatever positive means that we can. Just push forward. These four men remind us that great courage can lay in the hearts of the least valued among us. So, let's learn from this to equally value everyone in our spheres of influence. What an outstanding blessing! A totally unexpected discovery in the least expected place, their enemies' camp. Because when absolutely no one else would have dared to go anywhere near their enemy's camp, these four men simply set things into motion and chose to forcefully advance. Everyone was completely blown away by what God did. Our loving creator supernaturally intervened and put an end to all their miseries. The devastating famine ended abruptly, and all that we've learned so far should help all of us to determine afresh to get up and get going! Simply plug your faith into God's word and make your own move. Because there is always hope in God.

> Now faith is confidence in what we hope for and assurance about what we do not see (Hebrews 11:1, NIV).

> For in this hope we were saved. But hope that is seen is no hope at all. Who hopes for what they already have? (Romans 8:24, NIV).

Unleashing momentum can prove to be a catalyst for major breakthroughs.

To reiterate, we just simply have no idea what gems we might uncover when we decide to take action and move things forward. If we begin today, right now, to consistently apply this powerful principle to our lives, positive things will happen. You may have heard the idiom "too good to be true" being used to describe something that is so good that it's almost unbelievable. Well, this true story reminds us that with God, His miracles might indeed appear to be too good and still be true. In just one day, and with just one move, God made such an abundance of desperately needed provisions available for an entire country. The four lepers took the greatest risk of their lives, and their courage paid off big time!

The Lord knows how to rescue godly people from their trials (2 Peter 2:9, NLT).

Will you decide today to fully trust in God and draw from him the strength to forcefully advance?

Chapter Four

THE PROCESS

Let's take a brief look at some of the steps taken by these four men that led to their getting themselves and their entire country unstuck. First, they got up in their minds before they physically got moving.

> Why are we sitting here waiting to die? (2 Kings 7:3, NLT).

Secondly, they made the decision to do something to change their circumstances even though things looked completely hopeless.

> So, we might as well go out (2 Kings 7:4, NLT).

Thirdly, they followed their decisions with *prompt actions*, not allowing themselves to waver or talk themselves out of what they had decided.

> So they got up at dusk and went out (2 Kings 7:5, International Standard Version).

All of these steps led them to their enemy's camp; showing us the power that lies in simply choosing to forcefully advance even when we don't know what the final outcome of our choices will be. Against all odds, their actions brought a wonderful change to their own lives, as well as those of everyone else in their country. Remember these four men's courageous *actions* when all you feel like doing is curling up and giving up. It was their decision to set things in motion with the little strength that they all had left that resulted in everyone's coming out of this major disaster. "But someone may say, 'You [claim to] have faith and I have [good] works; show me your [alleged] faith without the works [if you can], and I will show you my faith by my works [that is, by what I do]'" James 2:18, AMP; brackets in the original).

When things look to you as if all the options that you have left are negative, will you consider creating momentum in your own circumstances, fully trusting God that He will work everything together for your good?

Place your trust in God and He will empower you by His grace to take decisive actions in the most unexpected ways. Start to apply what you've learned so far and push forward using whatever strength and means that you have left. God will surely not fail you if you trust in Him when you can't figure out what to do next.

"For the word of God will never fail" (Luke 1:37, NLT). Let these four men's journey be a source of inspiration and courage to reignite momentum in your own life and in your own way, and according to your level of faith. "For by the grace given me I say to every one of you: Do not think of yourself more highly than you ought, but rather think of yourself with sober judgment, in accordance with the faith God has distributed to each of you" (Romans 12:3, NIV).

> I am the LORD, the God of all the peoples of the world. Is anything too hard for me? (Jeremiah 32:27, NLT).

Instead of staying stuck, get up in your own mind first, and seize the momentum as they did. Take whatever actions are necessary to forcefully advance, regardless of the circumstances that you've been wrestling with. Your challenges will be completely different from the four lepers'. But out of His great love and mercy, God has promised to come to the rescue of all those who genuinely place their trust in Him.

> The LORD protects all those who love him (Psalm 145:20, NLT).

You might be facing ill health, bankruptcy, a relationship breakdown, an addiction, terrible living conditions, etc. But when it seems the most pointless to try to do anything about our negative circumstances or we're so discouraged from having tried and failed so many times before, I implore us to turn to God again for His help. Doing nothing but making excuses will not get us to where we need or want to be. So, start to seek practical and positive ways to move things forward in your life. The challenges that you're facing right now may look impossible to you to overcome, but they're not too big for God. As we go on with our discussion, we'll be learning a great deal from Israel's greatest king, David, on how to recover from repeated failures and major setbacks, and regain our momentum.

> Thanks be to God! He gives us the victory through our Lord Jesus Christ (1 Corinthians 15:57, NIV).

> I remain confident of this: I will see the goodness of the LORD in the land of the living (Psalm 27:13, NIV).

Are you willing to be a catalyst for a breakthrough for yourself and others—just as these four lepers were—that could bring blessings beyond your wildest dreams?

Chapter Five

Don't Stop Pedaling

I encourage all of us today to place our trust in God and exercise our faith. "For we walk by faith, not by sight [living our lives in a manner consistent with our confident belief in God's promises]" (2 Corinthians 5:7, AMP; brackets in the original). When faced with challenges, start to develop the habit of setting things into motion as quickly as possible. I understand that this will not at all be easy, especially when we have not been exercising our momentum muscle. But,

> *Stand your ground,* putting on the belt of truth and the body armor of God's righteousness (Ephesians 6:14, NIV; emphasis added).

> "Don't be afraid," he said, *"for you are very precious to God. Peace! Be encouraged! Be strong!"* As he spoke these words to me, I suddenly felt stronger and said to him, "Please speak to me, my lord, for you have strengthened me" Daniel 10:19, NLT; emphasis added).

As we go on, we will be learning more from many of God's people in the Bible who ignited momentum when all appeared to be lost. They were all led by Him to overwhelming success, despite things looking completely hopeless. These four brave lepers decided to take action and ended up receiving a massive miracle from God. No one else knew what had already taken place in their enemy's camp. Taking what looks to us like the greatest risk might, in fact, be the way out of our problems or be the way to experiencing one of God's miracles. The awful famine in Samaria finally came to an abrupt end, and we can imagine all of the screaming and shouting for joy that took place on that day. The scenes that unfolded can be pictured in all our minds, as people fell over each other with excitement to grab food and wolf it down. Suddenly gaining access to all these fresh supplies after having starved for so long, must have felt like a dream.

> When the Lord restored the fortunes of Zion,
>   we were like those who dreamed,
> our mouths were filled with laughter,
>   our tongues with songs of joy.
> Then it was said among the nations,
>   "The Lord has done great things for them."
> The Lord has done great things for us,
>   and we are filled with joy.
> Restore our fortunes, Lord,
>   like streams in the Negev.

> Those who sow with tears
> > will reap with songs of joy.
> Those who go out weeping,
> > carrying seed to sow,
> will return with songs of joy,
> > carrying sheaves with them
>
> (Psalms 126, NIV).

The thought might have occurred to you that somebody other than the four lepers could have discovered the provisions later on. You may be right about this, but we'll never know. But imagine that had these four lepers not chosen to set things in motion at the time that they did, many more people would have starved to death before the great discovery was finally made. And one could only hope that it would have been before all the supplies were spoilt or rotted. While the items were still fresh and usable, the great bounty that God made available had to be claimed quickly, because the people were in such dire need. So, someone had to be stirred up quickly to be desperate enough to go to the enemy's camp. In this case, it was the four out-of-their-minds—but courageous—lepers. I wonder who else would have dared to go anywhere near their dreaded enemy's camp after being under siege for so long. My thoughts are, "No one, that's who." Everyone would have rightly assumed that they would have been killed by these cruel people. But in a stunning turnaround, an entire nation was instantly and powerfully delivered from their enemies by God.

> *The nation of Israel received divine help to get unstuck, and this spectacular event was recorded for us all, so that we too can have faith in God's ability to rescue us more than in our enemy's ability to destroy us.*

The lepers were simply living their lives as best as they could under the circumstances in which they all found themselves; just as we try to do daily. Sometimes when we think that the worst is about to happen, the very best thing that could happens instead. Claude Pepper, an American author and statesman, made the following statement: "Life is like riding a bicycle: you don't fall off unless you stop pedaling." This is great encouragement to simply keep on pedaling. The power that lies in the simple step of creating or keeping your momentum cannot be overstated.

So, begin today to make spending quality time in God's presence a permanent part of your lifestyle, and the primary way that you ignite momentum daily. No matter how hopeless your current circumstances might look or how long you have been wrestling with them, start to take steps right now as these four men did, to push yourself forward. Big, exciting goals aren't always reached all at once. They're often achieved through a series of small steps, and each of those steps is a small triumph worth celebrating. Give yourself plenty of reasons to celebrate each day as you create momentum in big and small ways. Don't stay stuck for one moment longer. But give yourself plenty of time to recover from any major setbacks that you may already have experienced. And after a healthy amount of recovery time, based on your own unique needs and circumstances, begin to get yourself back up and on your feet again. Remember that God has promised to empower us by His grace when we stay closely connected to Him. Draw fresh strength from His powerful and unlimited resources today, and move your life forward.

God's love and power are inexhaustible.

If you will develop the habit of depending on Him, starting right now, He will surely help you to triumph over whatever you're currently facing. When we choose to create momentum, we will discover new answers to our problems that might not have been apparent to us at the start of our trials. They might not be as spectacular as the one we've just read, but each step that we take when we start to move things forward and choose to exercise our faith opens the door to receiving divine help. "And we know [with great confidence] that God [who is deeply concerned about us] causes all things to work together [as a plan] for good for those who love God, to those who are called according to His plan and purpose" (Romans 8:28, AMP; brackets in the original).

As mentioned earlier, momentum is an important key to nonstop progress. We must not allow our past failures, doubts, or fears to prevent us from experiencing God's abundant blessings. Let's get things moving. If we truly desire to continually experience success in our lives, it is vital that we start to exercise our faith in God, because as His believing children, "we now have this light shining in our hearts, but we ourselves are like fragile clay jars containing this great treasure. This makes it clear that our great power is from God, not from ourselves" (2 Corinthians 4:7, NLT). Let's do all that's within our power to set things in motion and head in the right direction: *forward*.

> So that your faith might not rest on human wisdom, but on God's power (1 Corinthians 2:5, NIV).

> Jesus looked at them intently and said, "Humanly speaking, it is impossible. But with God everything is possible" (Matthew 19:26, NLT).

Trust in God to work out the final outcome of your faith in Him together for our good and His glory.

Therefore, put on the complete armor of God, so that you will be able to *[successfully]* resist and stand your ground in the evil day [of danger], and having done everything [that the crisis demands], to stand firm [in your place, fully prepared, immovable, *victorious*]. So, stand firm *and* hold your ground, HAVING TIGHTENED THE WIDE BAND OF TRUTH (personal integrity, moral courage) AROUND YOUR WAIST and HAVING PUT ON THE BREASTPLATE OF RIGHTEOUSNESS (an upright heart) (Ephesians 6:13–14, AMP; emphasis added, brackets and capitalization in the original).

Starting from today, will you freshly commit to igniting or keeping up your momentum as a part of your lifestyle?

Chapter Six

Use These Key Ingredients

I first tasted lemonade as a child many years ago, and instantly fell in love with this tangy lemon drink. The recipe for lemonade usually calls for three basic ingredients: lemon, sugar, and water. If you use these ingredients, you'll end up with lemonade every single time, regardless of the individual adjustment for taste. Similarly, the recipe for success and creating nonstop progress is also simple, just these two principles:

Keep growing and keep going.

The need to stay curious and to keep growing has never been greater than in the times that we're living in. The advancements in modern technology just keep on exploding. All that we now have available at our fingertips via laptops, iPads, cellphones, and other devices affects nearly every area of our lives, because we use them for almost everything that we do. We cannot afford to be left behind, and there's always room for improvement. The former West German chancellor, Helmut Schmidt, once said, "The biggest room in the world is the room for improvement."

The many factors shaping our world today require nothing less than our focus and attention. Staying stuck in any area of our lives, while everything around us is evolving so fast, is not where we would want to be or stay. As new technology becomes available in the marketplace, familiarizing ourselves with the latest technology, and any other new things that are relevant to our own lives, is key to our achieving success. There is something to learn from every experience, even the negative ones. So, being willing to learn and grow helps us to create and keep up our momentum. But if you're tempted to give up before even trying, or start to feel overwhelmed by what I just said, remember this:

Always take things at your own pace.

Just keep on moving forward in all the positive ways that you can. As mentioned earlier, the primary way to do this is to nourish ourselves with God's word on a daily basis. Just as our physical bodies need nourishment daily to survive, our souls and spirits also need our attention in order to grow stronger in our faith and make continuous progress in all areas of our lives. Make it a habit to practice good spiritual protocols every day, no matter the difficulties you might encounter along the way. God's word is the solid foundation upon which we can securely and successfully build our lives.

Therefore, everyone who hears these words of mine and puts them into practice is like a *wise* man who built his house on the rock. The rain came down, the streams rose, and the winds blew and beat against that house; yet it did not fall, because it had its foundation on the rock. But everyone who hears these words of mine and does not put them into practice is like a foolish man who built his house on sand. The rain came down, the streams rose, and the winds blew and beat against that house, and it fell with a great crash (Matthew 7:24–27, NIV; emphasis added).

> For the protection of *wisdom* is like the protection of money, and the advantage of knowledge is that *wisdom* preserves the life of him who has it (Ecclesiastes 7:12, ESV; emphasis added).

> Asking God, the glorious Father of our Lord Jesus Christ, to give you *spiritual wisdom and insight* so that you might *grow* in your knowledge of God (Ephesians 1:17, NLT; emphasis added).

The scriptures encourage us not to feed our minds on trash, but to stay connected to and hungry for God's word.

> A wise person is hungry for knowledge, while the fool feeds on trash (Proverbs 15:14, NLT).
>
> Intelligent people are always ready to learn. Their ears are open for knowledge (Proverbs 18:15, NLT).

Not only do we need to keep growing in order to experience progress in our lives, we also need to *keep on going*. This prevents us from declining into laziness and lack of application or stagnancy. While enjoying our successes we must not rest on our laurels, and if we experience failure we must never quit or give up. American explorer, Robert Peary once said, "*The time to prepare for your next expedition is when you have just returned from a successful trip.*"

We're also promised in God's word that if we place our trust in Him, He will lead and guide us in all our ways as we *proceed*. "I will instruct you and teach you in the way you should go; I will counsel you with my loving eye on you" (Psalm 32:8, NIV). So, don't allow any doubts or fears to prevent you from experiencing the rich and satisfying life that God has in mind for each one of us. "The thief's purpose is to steal and kill and destroy. My purpose is to give them a rich and satisfying life" (John 10:10, NLT). Start today, right now, to move your own situation forward by reconnecting with God.

> For every child of God defeats this evil world, and we achieve this victory through our faith (1 John 5:4, NLT).

We can start to create momentum in our lives in very simple ways, like going for a walk. Many experts tell us that engaging in some form of physical activity when we're feeling down or stuck is a helpful way to move toward recovery. This can help us to reignite our momentum when things look bleak or we feel like we're all out of options. Does everything around you only appear to confirm your imminent defeat? Or are you just too tired from trying to put up a fight for so long? If so, please take heart and gain courage from the four lepers' story, and get things back into motion in your own life. Keep in mind that remaining in the parked position will just not get us to where we would want to be.

Operate within your own level of faith.

Each one of us can become a catalyst for a breakthrough—not only for ourselves, but for many others—despite the many unique and varied situations that human beings might find themselves faced with. Unusual answers may have been prepared ahead by God, but they can only be discovered if we get going. So, when things look bleak to us, we must take courage and prompt action. God has repeatedly promised to give us the strength that we need to get ourselves unstuck.

> What shall we say about such wonderful things as these? If God is for us, who can ever be against us? (Romans 8:31, NLT).

> Look straight ahead, and fix your eyes on what lies before you. Mark out a straight path for your feet; stay on the safe path. Don't get sidetracked; keep your feet from following evil (Proverbs 4:25–27, NIV).

All that we've done so far to stay afloat will not be in vain. Because creating and keeping up our momentum will always be the right thing to do in all circumstances. So, don't give up, because smaller victories can pave the way for bigger ones. We will be learning more about this during our discussion. But for right now, decide to intentionally set things in motion in your own life. Trust God that He will show you the way out of your direst needs. Our creator is ready, willing, and able to take care of all our needs. He is the one who lights up our paths. Are you willing to place your complete trust in Him?

> Jesus answered, "I am the way and the truth and the life. No one comes to the Father except through me" (John 14:6, NIV).

> The Word gave life to everything that was created, and his life brought light to everyone (John 1:4, NIV).

> Your word is a lamp to guide my feet and a light for my path (Psalm 119:105, NLT).

Things did not at all look good for the four lepers. But they still chose to *proceed* and get unstuck from their appalling circumstances. God has promised us that the processes that we go through will be worked together for our good. "For in him we live and move and exist" (Acts 17:28, NLT). As unique as your own circumstances might be, don't give up. Seize the momentum right now. This principle, if consistently applied, can transform our lives. Remember that many people on our planet may be experiencing some of the same things that you might be going through, and the gems you might uncover could bring answers to long-standing problems for yourself and others that no one else knew anything about.

> No, dear brothers and sisters, I have not achieved it, but I focus on this one thing: Forgetting the past and looking forward to what lies ahead (Philippians 3:13, NLT).

Choosing to move things forward despite not having all our needs met yet was powerfully illustrated by the Lord

Jesus in the account of how He miraculously multiplied five loaves of bread and two fish to feed a multitude of people.

> When Jesus landed and saw a large crowd, he had compassion on them, because they were like sheep without a shepherd. So he began teaching them many things. By this time it was late in the day, so his disciples came to him. "This is a remote place," they said, "and it's already very late. Send the people away so that they can go to the surrounding countryside and villages and buy themselves something to eat." But he answered, "You give them something to eat. "They said to him, "That would take more than half a year's wages! Are we to go and spend that much on bread and give it to them to eat?" "How many loaves do you have?" he asked. "Go and see." When they found out, they said, "Five—and two fish." Then Jesus directed them to have all the people sit down in groups on the green grass. So they sat down in groups of hundreds and fifties.
>
> *Taking the five loaves and the two fish and looking up to heaven, he gave thanks and broke the loaves.*
>
> Then he gave them to his disciples to distribute to the people. He also divided the two fish

among them all. They all ate and were satisfied, and the disciples picked up twelve basketfuls of broken pieces of bread and fish. The number of the men who had eaten was five thousand (Mark 6:34–44, NIV; emphasis added).

The following observations about this incident are from one of my previous books titled *All Will Be Well*. You will notice that when confronted with such a great need, Jesus' first action was to keep everyone in order by asking His disciples to organize those present into small groups. This is another key to obtaining God's help. When faced with seemingly insurmountable odds. Don't focus on the problem and panic. Nothing useful can emerge from fear, panic, and disorderliness. Instead, initiate sensible actions toward solving the problem. After settling everyone down, Jesus then looked up to heaven and prayed. This is also another great key to receiving divine help.

> *Always show your gratitude to God for what you already possess, no matter how small it might be compared to the size of your need. This will open the doors to divine blessings.*

"Let us come into his presence with thanksgiving" (Psalm 95:2, ESV). Although Jesus was expected to meet this sizable responsibility with nothing but a few loaves of bread and two fish, He didn't grumble or complain. He first thanked God for what He already had, although it must have been obvious to all who were present that five loaves and two fish could never satisfy such a large crowd. Some members of his audience probably thought that he was joking. Yet Jesus knew that God would do the impossible out of His great love. Giving thanks to God for what we already possess creates an atmosphere in which not enough can become more than enough, regardless of the pressures that we might be under.

> I lift my eyes to you, O God, enthroned in heaven (Psalm 123:1, NLT).

After connecting with God through His prayers, Jesus instructed his disciples to *proceed* and distribute the little amount of food that they had. Even though it was quite clear that it wouldn't be enough to meet the sizeable need at hand. But God's miraculous provision was once again revealed as the disciples created *momentum* by giving out the very little food that they had. The five thousand men who were fed on that day did not include the women and children. So, it might have been closer to over twenty thousand people who were fed through God's supernatural provision. After the miracle had taken place and the people had eaten until they were full, the crumbs that were left over and gathered by the disciples were enough to fill twelve baskets! Truly, life in all its abundance! "If you are willing and obedient, you will eat the good things of the land" (Isaiah 1:19, NIV).

We must remember that the abundant blessings that God has in store for us will not manifest themselves in our lives until we first place our unwavering trust in Him.

> When you ask, you must believe and not doubt, because the one who doubts is like a wave of the sea, blown and tossed by the wind. That person should not expect to receive anything from the Lord. Such a person is double-minded and unstable in all they do (James 1:6–8, NIV).

> God is faithful [He is reliable, trustworthy and ever true to His promise—He can be depended on], and through Him you were called into fellowship with His Son, Jesus Christ our Lord (1 Corinthians 1:9, AMP; brackets in the original).

> I know the LORD is always with me. I will not be shaken, for he is right beside me (Psalm 16:8, NLT).

Faced with such a massive crowd's needs, Jesus simply *proceeded* to take the necessary *actions*. Starting with thanksgiving and prayers to God. Whenever going back is not an option and going forward seems impossible, simply plug your faith into God and set things into motion in whatever positive ways that you can, using whatever strength or resources that you have left. We do not need to have all the answers to our problems before choosing to do something about them. Forcefully advance. Just as the four lepers that we read about earlier did, refuse to stay stuck no matter what the obstacles in your way might be. On many occasions in the Bible, people just like us were faced with seemingly insurmountable odds. When they could not figure the way out on their own, they simply turned to God for help and were able to turn things around.

God made ways where there were no ways!

> And what more shall I say? I do not have time to tell about Gideon, Barak, Samson, and Jephthah, about David and Samuel and the prophets, who through faith conquered kingdoms, administered justice, and gained what was promised; who shut the mouths of lions, quenched the fury of the flames, and escaped the edge of the sword; whose weakness was turned to strength; and who became powerful in battle and routed foreign armies (Hebrews 11:32–34, NIV).

Here are some more of God's promises for us to draw fresh strength from.

"They will fight against you but will not overcome you, for I am with you and will rescue you," declares the LORD (Jeremiah 1:19, NIV).

Through you we push back our enemies; through your name we trample our foes. I put no trust in my bow, my sword does not bring me victory; but you give us victory over our enemies, you put our adversaries to shame (Psalm 44:5–7, NIV).

Thanks be to God! He gives us the victory through our Lord Jesus Christ (1 Corinthians 15:57, NIV).

Will you start to apply this powerful principle of unleashing momentum in your own life, starting today, right now?

Chapter Seven

Don't Stay Disheartened

I want to be as sensitive as possible in this part of our discussion because it deals with the most painful human experience, death. It is humankind's last enemy. All of us human beings are forced to face our own mortality when our loved ones, coworkers, or even strangers sadly pass away. I believe that losing a loved one is probably the most challenging emotional experience to overcome. While I am not a grief counselor or a psychologist, I take all the counsel and truths that I am asking us to apply to our lives from the scriptures.

> Oh, *the depth of the riches and wisdom and knowledge of God!* (Romans 11:33, ESV; emphasis added).

> For a child is born to us, a son is given to us. The government will rest on his shoulders. And he will be called: *Wonderful Counselor*, Mighty God, Everlasting Father, Prince of Peace (Isaiah 9:6, NLT; emphasis added).

> This also comes from the LORD of hosts; he is *wonderful in counsel* and excellent in wisdom, (Isaiah 28:29, ESV; emphasis added).

> "I have *counsel and sound wisdom*; I have insight; I have strength" (Proverbs 8:14, ESV; emphasis added).

God's Holy Spirit residing within all His believing children is our counselor, advocate, and comforter. He empowers us to recover from this severest of life's blows.

> But the Helper (Comforter, Advocate, Intercessor—*Counselor, Strengthener*, Standby), the Holy Spirit, whom the Father will send in My name [in My place, to represent Me and act on My behalf], He will teach you all things. And He will help you remember everything that I have told you (John 14:26, AMP; brackets in the original).

In my previous books, I have drawn many valuable lessons from the life of King David of Israel. His life has been depicted in so many stories, movies, and books. Especially the part about an unforgettable encounter that David had as a young man with a Philistine giant by the name of Goliath. This happened before he became the king (see 1 Samuel 17). He won an epic victory over Goliath, and later went on to become Israel's king, after overcoming many other difficulties. But most of us would not have been able to recover from some of the other terrible experiences that King David later had to overcome in his life. And while some of the blows that he experienced were self-inflicted.—either due to his own negligence, disobedience, or lust—we can still draw so many lessons from King David's life about unleashing the powerful key of momentum.

Through his decisions and choices, this impressive man shows us how to overcome adversity, and that flawed human beings like ourselves can recover from some of life's most devastating losses.

> For though the righteous fall seven times, they rise again, but the wicked stumble when calamity strikes (Proverbs 24:16, NIV).

King David in my mind is the *King of Momentum*, because whatever situation that he faced, he would successfully reignite and keep up his momentum. He had a very close relationship with God and made worshipping Him his and his nation's top priority (see 1 Chronicles 16). Here also are some of the words penned by David that document his great love for God and the passion with which he sought after Him.

> A Psalm of David; when he was in the wilderness of Judah. O God, You are my God; with

> deepest longing I will seek You; My soul [my life, my very self] thirsts for You, my flesh longs and sighs for You, In a dry and weary land where there is no water (Psalm 63:1, AMP; brackets in the original).
>
> I will exalt You, my God, O King, and [with gratitude and submissive wonder] I will bless Your name forever and ever (Psalm 145:1, AMP; brackets in the original).

It was his intimate relationship with God that enabled King David to master the skill of keeping things moving even when he was dealt life's toughest blows. He suffered more than a few of these. One of the saddest episodes, and my least favorite story to read in the Bible, was when King David lusted after a married woman and conspired to have her husband killed so that he could have her (see 2 Samuel 11). David had previously been described as "a man after God's own heart" in both 1 Samuel 13:14 and Acts 13:22. And what was just as egregious as King David's awful actions was his complete denial of his sins and unwillingness to repent.

King David had somehow lost the ability to recognize the extent to which he had fallen, and he refused to take any responsibility for the great evil that he had done. The woman that he forcibly took was named Bathsheba, and her husband's name was Uriah the Hittite.

After having Uriah killed, David went ahead and took Bathsheba as his own wife. This was despite the fact that he already had many wives; incidentally, another thing strictly prohibited by God.

> The king, moreover, must not acquire great numbers of horses for himself or make the people return to Egypt to get more of them, for the LORD has told you, "You are not to go back that way again." The king must not take many wives for himself, because they will turn his heart away from the LORD. And he must not accumulate large amounts of wealth in silver and gold for himself (Deuteronomy 17:16, NIV; 17:17, NLT).

"Loving God means keeping his commandments, and his commandments are not burdensome" (1 John 5:3, NLT). God's commands are to be obeyed. They are not suggestions. They are written in order to protect, guide, and train us to live our lives successfully.

> All Scripture is inspired by God and is useful to teach us what is true and to make us realize what is wrong in our lives. It corrects us when we are wrong and teaches us to do what is right (2 Timothy 3:16, NLT).

Although King David had received so many privileges from God, and had previously been very close to Him, he flagrantly disobeyed God's commands in this and some other, yet to be discussed, instances. But after Bathsheba became David's wife, here is what happened:

> When Uriah's wife heard that her husband was dead, she mourned for him. When the period of mourning was over, David sent for her and brought her to the palace, and she became one of his wives. Then she gave birth to a son. But the Lord was displeased with what David had done. So the Lord sent Nathan the prophet to tell David this story: "There were two men in a certain town. One was rich, and one was poor. The rich man owned a great many sheep and cattle. The poor man owned nothing but one little lamb he had bought. He raised that little lamb, and it grew up with his children. It ate from the man's own plate and drank from his cup. He cuddled it in his arms like a baby daughter. One day a guest arrived at the home of the rich man. But instead of killing an animal from his own flock or herd, he took the poor man's lamb and killed it and prepared it for his guest." David was furious. "As surely as the Lord lives," he vowed, "any man who would do such a thing deserves to die! He must repay four lambs to the poor man for the one he stole and for having no pity." Then Nathan said to

David, "You are that man! The Lord, the God of Israel, says: I anointed you king of Israel and saved you from the power of Saul.

"I gave you your master's house and his wives and the kingdoms of Israel and Judah. And if that had not been enough, I would have given you much, much more. Why, then, have you despised the word of the Lord and done this horrible deed? For you have murdered Uriah the Hittite with the sword of the Ammonites and stolen his wife. From this time on, your family will live by the sword because you have despised me by taking Uriah's wife to be your own. This is what the Lord says: Because of what you have done, I will cause your own household to rebel against you. I will give your wives to another man before your very eyes, and he will go to bed with them in public view. You did it secretly, but I will make this happen to you openly in the sight of all Israel." Then David confessed to Nathan, "I have sinned against the Lord." Nathan replied, "Yes, but the Lord has forgiven you, and you won't die for this sin. Nevertheless, because you have shown utter contempt for the word of the Lord by doing this, your child will die."

David begged God to spare the child. He went without food and lay all night on the bare ground. The elders of his household pleaded with him to get up and eat with them, but he refused. Then on the seventh day the child died. David's advisers were afraid to tell him. "He wouldn't listen to reason while the child was ill," they said. "What drastic thing will he do when we tell him the child is dead?" When David saw them whispering, he realized what had happened. "Is the child dead?" he asked. "Yes," they replied, "he is dead." Then David got up from the ground, washed himself, put on lotions and changed his clothes. He went to the Tabernacle and worshiped the Lord. After that, he returned to the palace and was served food and ate. His advisers were amazed. "We don't understand you," they told him. "While the child was still living, you wept and refused to eat. But now that the child is dead, you have stopped your mourning and are eating again." David replied, "I fasted and wept while the child was alive, for I said, 'Perhaps the Lord will be gracious to me and let the child live.' But why should I fast when he is dead? Can I bring him back again? I will go to him one day, but he cannot return to me." Then David comforted Bathsheba, his wife, and slept with her. She became pregnant and gave birth to a son, and David named him Solomon. The

Lord loved the child and sent word through Nathan the prophet that they should name him Jedidiah (which means "beloved of the Lord"), as the Lord had commanded (2 Samuel 11:26–27, 12:1–14, 16–25, NLT).

As we just read, God is extremely merciful. We already ought to know this. Because we're also recipients of His great mercy and love. When He sacrificed His only begotten son on the cross for our sins. Jesus took the full punishment for our sins, and satisfied God's righteous requirements for justice, while obtaining a full pardon for us. "He is so rich in kindness and grace that he purchased our freedom with the blood of his Son and forgave our sins" (Ephesians 1:7 NLT). Our loving creator is the judge of the whole earth and the one ultimately responsible for ensuring that justice is perfectly carried out. This includes justice for the murdered man, Uriah. The way that God handled King David's epic failure demonstrated to all that when God forgives us, He truly does so completely. How merciful He was toward David as first evidenced by not having him immediately put to death. God's law states this:

> If a man commits adultery with another man's wife—with the wife of his neighbor—both the adulterer and the adulteress are to be put to death (Leviticus 20:10, NIV).

Secondly, by granting David and Bathsheba another son, Solomon—who became the king after him, and one of the wealthiest kings in history—God makes it clear that He would not hold this sin against any of David's future offspring with Bathsheba. Solomon would later shed great glory upon David's name. But even more astonishing is the fact that God allowed His only begotten son Jesus Christ, the Savior of the world, to be a direct descendant of King David.

> For the Scriptures clearly state that the Messiah will be born of the royal line of David, in Bethlehem, the village where King David was born (John 7:42, NLT).

While we might think that God is sometimes slow in bringing about justice, He assures us that He will act on our and other people's behalf when it is His right time.

> At the time I have planned, I will bring justice against the wicked (Psalm 75:2, NLT).

> Dear friends, never take revenge. Leave that to the righteous anger of God. For the Scriptures say, "I will take revenge; I will pay them back," says the LORD (Romans 12:19, NLT).

> For he has set a day for judging the world with justice by the man he has appointed, and he proved to everyone who this is by raising him from the dead (Acts 17:31, NLT).

> He rules the world in righteousness and judges the peoples with equity (Psalm 9:8, NIV).

After King David had been corrected and fully pardoned by God, he genuinely repented from his sins, as documented in a Psalm that he wrote following this horrible incident.

> Have mercy on me, O God,
>   according to your unfailing love;
> according to your great compassion
>   blot out my transgressions.
> Wash away all my iniquity
>   and cleanse me from my sin.
> For I know my transgressions,
>   and my sin is always before me.
> Against you, you only, have I sinned
>   and done what is evil in your sight;
> so you are right in your verdict
>   and justified when you judge.
> Surely I was sinful at birth,
>   sinful from the time my mother conceived me.

Yet you desired faithfulness even in the womb;
    you taught me wisdom in that secret place.
Cleanse me with hyssop, and I will be clean;
    wash me, and I will be whiter than snow.
Let me hear joy and gladness;
    let the bones you have crushed rejoice.
Hide your face from my sins
    and blot out all my iniquity.
Create in me a pure heart, O God,
    and renew a steadfast spirit within me.
Do not cast me from your presence
    or take your Holy Spirit from me.
Restore to me the joy of your salvation
    and grant me a willing spirit, to sustain me.
Then I will teach transgressors your ways,
    so that sinners will turn back to you.
Deliver me from the guilt of bloodshed, O God,
    you who are God my Savior,
    and my tongue will sing of your righteousness.
Open my lips, Lord,
    and my mouth will declare your praise.
You do not delight in sacrifice, or I would bring it;
    you do not take pleasure in burnt offerings.
My sacrifice, O God, is a broken spirit;
    a broken and contrite heart
    you, God, will not despise.

> May it please you to prosper Zion,
> > to build up the walls of Jerusalem
> Then you will delight in the sacrifices of the
> > righteous,
> > in burnt offerings offered whole;
> > then bulls will be offered on your altar
> (Psalm 51:1–19, NLT).

A great and powerful leader of his time. After offering the no-excuses, heartfelt apology to God for all his wrongdoings, David then begins to show all of us how to reignite momentum after a great fall. He started this by taking clear steps to recover from his grief and loss after losing his first child with Bathsheba. David as we learned earlier was a genuine worshipper of God. So first, he changed from his mourning clothes and posture and went into God's presence to worship Him.

> David noticed that his attendants were whispering among themselves, and he realized the child was dead. 'Is the child dead?' he asked. 'Yes,' they replied, 'he is dead.' *Then David got up from the ground. After he had washed, put on lotions and changed his clothes, he went into the house of the Lord and worshiped* (2 Samuel 12:19–20, NIV; emphasis added).

This is an essential key to moving forward after the process of grieving, in order for us to experience fuller recoveries, because the strength to successfully overcome life's most difficult trials and adversities can only be received from God. The scriptures tell us this.

> Your roots will grow down into God's love and keep you strong" (Ephesians 3:17, NLT).

We also learn this from another man in the Bible, whose name was Job, when he was suddenly confronted with great calamity. He was the wealthiest man of his times and in his region. But one day, he suddenly lost everything that he owned and all ten of his children. His unquantifiable grief would be unimaginable to most of us. But as we read that King David did, Job also responded to these catastrophic losses by going into God's presence and losing himself in worship as he mourned.

> Job got up and tore his robe and shaved his head. Then he fell to the ground in worship and said: "Naked I came from my mother's womb, and naked I will depart. The Lord gave and the Lord has taken away; may the name of the Lord be praised." In all this, Job did not sin by charging God with wrongdoing (Job 1:20–22, NLT).

David continued to reignite his momentum when he took the following additional steps. "Then he went to his own house, and at his request they served him food, and he ate" (2 Samuel 12:20, NIV). David might not at all have felt like eating. Many people who have gone through the loss of a loved one sometimes lose all their appetite for food, interest in keeping up personal hygiene routines, etc. But King David teaches us to intentionally request and eat some food. Because he understood that his physical body needed to recover from all the trauma that he had been through. So, whether he felt like eating or not, he chose to do so, in order to be strong enough to do whatever needed to be done next.

After he had finished eating and gained some strength, David reshaped his thinking by making a transformational statement in order to cast a new vision for his and Bathsheba's future.

> His attendants asked him, "Why are you acting this way? While the child was alive, you fasted and wept, but now that the child is dead, you get up and eat!" He answered, "While the child was still alive, I fasted and wept. I thought, 'Who knows? The Lord may be gracious to me and let the child live.' But now that he is dead, why should I go on fasting? Can I bring him back again? *I will go to him, but he will not return to me*" (2 Samuel 12:19–22, NIV; emphasis added).

King David also took on the full responsibility for initiating the reconciliation process between himself and the woman whose family and life he had destroyed, Bathsheba. He had been the aggressor and primary offender in this situation because all the power was on his side as the sovereign at the time. David did not hide from his obligations both as a husband and leader. He reached out to Bathsheba, and with God's help, after spending time in worship, was able to reconcile with her. I believe that this reconciliation was only made possible because David had first gone into God's presence to worship and seek His help.

He restored his broken relationship with God first, before going to see his wife, Bathsheba. David trusted in his faith and knowledge that God is full of loving mercy and compassion, and that He had completely forgiven all of his sins. As I mentioned earlier, we're told to come boldly into God's presence and ask for help whenever we need it. God granted King David the grace, to clear out all his spiritual, emotional, and any other baggage so that he could *move things forward* and reignite momentum with his new wife Bathsheba.

> Then David comforted Bathsheba, his wife, and slept with her. She became pregnant and gave birth to a son, and David named him Solomon. The Lord loved the child and sent word through Nathan the prophet that they should name him

Jedidiah (which means "beloved of the Lord"), as the Lord had commanded (2 Samuel 12:24–25, NLT).

I believe that it was the grace that God granted to both of them that enabled Bathsheba to genuinely forgive David and put the past behind her. In spite of all that had happened—which included the loss of her loyal husband, Uriah, and her first child—Bathsheba chose to create new momentum with David by forgiving him.

> *They both got unstuck from this national scandal after receiving God's forgiveness and restoration. Their family would go on to be fruitful and successful.*

We learn from all these events that even though King David and Bathsheba had a whole lot of the heaviest sort of spiritual and emotional baggage to get rid of, they both chose to forcefully advance to move their lives forward. Bathsheba would live long enough to see their son Solomon take his father's throne and become one of the wealthiest kings in history, fulfilling their God-given destinies that David's sins almost sabotaged.

Another essential part of reigniting momentum is getting back to our normal duties as quickly and as much as possible. King David took this last important step by returning to work. Incidentally, it was his not being at work when he was supposed to be that had started this entire most unfortunate episode.

> In the spring of the year, *when kings normally go out to war*, David sent Joab and the Israelite army to fight the Ammonites. They destroyed the Ammonite army and laid siege to the city of Rabbah. However, David stayed behind in Jerusalem. Late one afternoon, after his midday rest, David got out of bed and was walking on the roof of the palace. As he looked out over the city, he noticed a woman of unusual beauty taking a bath. He sent someone to find out who she was, and he was told, "She is Bathsheba, the daughter of Eliam and the wife of Uriah the Hittite." Then David sent messengers to get her; and when she came to the palace, he slept with her . . . .Then she returned home (2 Samuel 11:1–4, NLT; emphasis added).

David went back to fight the war that he had lazily left to his general, Joab. This is another extremely important aspect of reclaiming victory in our own lives.

> Meanwhile, Joab was fighting against Rabbah, the capital of Ammon, and he captured the royal fortifications. Joab sent messengers to tell David, "I have fought against Rabbah and

captured its water supply. Now bring the rest of the army and capture the city. Otherwise, I will capture it and get credit for the victory." So David gathered the rest of the army and went to Rabbah, and he fought against it and captured it. David removed the crown from the king's head and it was placed on his own head. The crown was made of gold and set with gems, and it weighed seventy-five pounds. David took a vast amount of plunder from the city. He also made slaves of the people of Rabbah and forced them to labor with saws, iron picks, and iron axes, and to work in the brick kilns. That is how he dealt with the people of all the Ammonite towns. Then David and all the army returned to Jerusalem (2 Samuel 11:26–31, NIV).

We must learn to release our past failures to God as King David did. Because He truly has pardoned us when we genuinely repented of them. David would go on to expand his nation's territory by choosing to not stay stuck at home and wallowing in self-loathing. Nor did he fear losing the war as a punishment from God because this was the same war in which he had conspired with Joab to murder Uriah. A true worshipper of God, David believed and trusted in God's forgiveness. Because only a person who truly had faith in God could have dared to go back to the same location and battle and still expect victory after all that had happened. "For as the heavens are high above the earth, so great is His lovingkindness toward those who fear and worship Him [with awe-filled respect and deepest reverence]. As far as the east is from the west, So far has He removed our transgressions from us" (Psalm 103:11–12, AMP; brackets in the original). Letting go of the past is a must for all of us. Because we cannot do anything to change it. We can only make our mark on the future.

> Brothers and sisters, I do not consider myself yet to have taken hold of it. But one thing I do: Forgetting what is behind and straining toward what is ahead. I press on toward the goal to win the prize for which God has called me heavenward in Christ Jesus. (Philippians 3:13–14, NIV).

> *Allowing the guilt and regrets of yesteryear to hold us back or captive will bring our momentum to a screeching halt. We cannot go anywhere or be a blessing to anyone if we choose to dwell in and on our past.*

As God empowers us, we must get ourselves unstuck, as King David did, and set things back into motion to move our lives forward. It is often said that we must get back on the horse after falling off. During our discussion, we will see the principle of igniting and keeping up our momentum play out over and over again in King David's life and the lives of many of God's people in the Bible. Their stories were recorded for us so that we would not give up, but be encouraged to go on with our own lives.

> Therefore, since we are surrounded by such a huge crowd of witnesses to the life of faith, let us strip off every weight that slows us down, especially the sin that so easily trips us up. And let us run with endurance the race God has set before us. We do this by keeping our eyes on Jesus, the champion who initiates and perfects our faith. Because of the joy awaiting him, he endured the cross, disregarding its shame. Now he is seated in the place of honor beside God's throne (Hebrews 12:1–2, NLT).

This very sad incident in King David's life is an important reminder for us to never get lukewarm in our relationship with God. We must also stay vigilant lest we fall. His passion for God had waned, and this opened the door for the wrong sort of passion to take a strong hold of him. Reignite your momentum. Act on this powerful truth today and start to move your own life forward.

If you have failed greatly in your own life, are you willing to receive fresh strength from God to get past it?

Chapter Eight

INFINITE GRACE OVERCOMES UGLY CONSEQUENCES

As we learned from King David's life, God is merciful and compassionate, "Because of the LORD's great love, we are not consumed, for his compassions never fail. They are new every morning; great is your faithfulness" (Lamentations 3:22–23, NIV). Human history is very messy. The original sin of the first two human beings whom God created—Adam and Eve—resulted in terrible consequences that affect our lives today in ways that are well known to us all (see Genesis 1–3). The evils that plague our planet today are all the direct consequences of the fall of human beings.

After disobeying God's commands, Adam and Eve inherited Satan's sinful nature, and then passed it down to all of their posterity. Pain, suffering, and death have since plagued our planet. But because of His great love and mercy, God sacrificed His only begotten son, Jesus Christ, on the cross for all of our past, present, and future sins. Our loving creator is unwavering in His commitment to redeem human beings and have them in His family forever. He continues to demonstrate His unfathomable love in all that He does for us.

> For my Father's will is that everyone who looks to the Son and believes in him shall have eternal life, and I will raise them up at the last day (John 6:40, NIV).

> For the wages of sin is death, but the free gift of God [that is, His remarkable, overwhelming gift of grace to believers] is eternal life in Christ Jesus our Lord (Romans 6:23, AMP; brackets in the original).

In our day and age, the abundance of technological advancements has made the Bible readily and freely available to almost everyone on the planet. There are simply almost no excuses left for anyone to remain ignorant of God's commands. They have been written down for us so that we can *know* and *do* them, and navigate our lives successfully.

> For everything that was written in the past was written to teach us, so that through the endurance taught in the Scriptures and the encouragement they provide we might have hope (Romans 15:4, NIV).

> All Scripture is inspired by God and is useful to teach us what is true and to make us realize what is wrong in our lives. It corrects us when we are wrong and teaches us to do what is right (2 Timothy 3:16, NLT).

God, however, does not sugarcoat any of the terrible consequences of human beings' rebelliousness and atrocious behaviors. After we have received God's free pardon, it is of vital importance to know that not all the *consequences* of human beings' sinful choices will be prevented or removed by God. This is because He is the righteous judge of the whole earth, and He must not prevent justice from taking place. For an example, if a person commits an act of fraud and later repents to God, they will be completely forgiven by Him. But by the law, when that person is arrested for their crimes, they will have to pay for what they have stolen, and possibly go to prison. These are the rightful consequences of their sin.

> Righteousness and justice are the foundation of your throne. Unfailing love and truth walk before you as attendants (Psalm 89:14, NLT).

> "For the LORD is our judge, our lawgiver, and our king. He will care for us and save us (Isaiah 33:22, NLT).

God does completely forgive all our sins when we genuinely confess and repent from them. He is with us no matter what we have to go through as direct or indirect consequences of our sins, e.g., court hearings, prison time, etc.

> If we confess our sins to him, he is faithful and just to forgive us our sins and to cleanse us from all wickedness, (1 John 1:9, NLT).

> Finally, I confessed all my sins to you and stopped trying to hide my guilt. I said to myself, 'I will confess my rebellion to the LORD.' And you forgave me! All my guilt is gone (Psalm 32:5, NLT).

So, we must place our trust in God to deal with all the consequences of our choices. He will cause everything to work together for our good and the good of all those who have been negatively impacted by our choices. "And we know [with great confidence] that God [who is deeply concerned about us] causes all things to work together [as a plan] for good for those who love God, to those who are called according to His plan and purpose" (Romans 8:28, AMP; brackets in the original). Governmental authorities have been placed on the earth to protect people, their relationships, and their assets. The attitude of heart that we show toward any negative consequences that we might have to suffer will also be proof of our genuine repentance.

> Produce fruit in keeping with repentance (Luke 3:8, NIV).

> So, produce fruit that is consistent with repentance [demonstrating new behavior that proves a change of heart, and a conscious decision to turn away from sin] (Matthew 3:8, AMP; brackets in the original).

Our heavenly father is not a human being, and His ways and thoughts are much higher than ours.

> For just as the heavens are higher than the earth, so my ways are higher than your ways and my thoughts higher than your thoughts. The rain and snow come down from the heavens and stay on the ground to water the earth. They cause the grain to grow, producing seed for the farmer and bread for the hungry. It is the same with my word. I send it out, and it always produces fruit. It will accomplish all I want it to, and it will prosper everywhere I send it (Isaiah 55:9–11, AMP).

But the saddest thing of all is that many people still do not know about or believe in God's forgiveness for all their sins. Some also actually erroneously attribute the terrible things done by fallen human beings to God Himself. Many have rejected God's offer of forgiveness. While others deny His existence. Evil continues to plague our world, while souls are being lost every day through their unbelief. A great number of people will leave the earth and enter eternity without ever having placed their trust in Jesus Christ's sacrifice for their sins. Blaming God for the sad consequences of human beings' sins is the wrong way to go.

> *God is the source of our lives and blessings. He is the one ultimately responsible for avenging the wrongs that take place on the earth.*

As discussed earlier, David had been completely forgiven of all his sins by God. He would not have to die as required by the law. But there would be some horrible consequences that his evil actions would bring upon his family and nation. Do you still recall some of the words spoken by the prophet Nathan to King David when he was sent by God to correct him after his grave error? Let's refresh our memory.

> "Why, then, have you despised the word of the Lord and done this horrible deed? For you have murdered Uriah the Hittite with the sword of the Ammonites and stolen his wife. From this

time on, your family will live by the sword because you have despised me by taking Uriah's wife to be your own. This is what the Lord says: Because of what you have done, I will cause your own household to rebel against you. I will give your wives to another man before your very eyes, and he will go to bed with them in public view. You did it secretly, but I will make this happen to you openly in the sight of all Israel." Then David confessed to Nathan, "I have sinned against the Lord." Nathan replied, "Yes, but the Lord has forgiven you, and you won't die for this sin. Nevertheless, because you have shown utter contempt for the word of the Lord by doing this, your child will die" (2 Samuel 12:9–14, NLT).

After David and Bathsheba's first child died, the next series of disastrous consequences began with one of King David's children named Amnon. The young man had closely observed his father's poor example and his attempts to cover them up. So, he did the unimaginable in David's own family.

> In the course of time, Amnon son of David fell in love with Tamar, the beautiful sister of Absalom son of David. Amnon became so obsessed with his sister Tamar that he made himself ill. She was a virgin, and it seemed

impossible for him to do anything to her. Now Amnon had an adviser named Jonadab son of Shimeah, David's brother. Jonadab was a very shrewd man. He asked Amnon, "Why do you, the king's son, look so haggard morning after morning? Won't you tell me?" Amnon said to him, "I'm in love with Tamar, my brother Absalom's sister." "Go to bed and pretend to be ill," Jonadab said. "When your father comes to see you, say to him, 'I would like my sister Tamar to come and give me something to eat. Let her prepare the food in my sight so I may watch her and then eat it from her hand.'" So, Amnon lay down and pretended to be ill. When the king came to see him, Amnon said to him, "I would like my sister Tamar to come and make some special bread in my sight, so I may eat from her hand."

David sent word to Tamar at the palace: "Go to the house of your brother Amnon and prepare some food for him." So Tamar went to the house of her brother Amnon, who was lying down. She took some dough, kneaded it, made the bread in his sight and baked it. Then she took the pan and served him the bread, but he refused to eat. "Send everyone out of here," Amnon said. So everyone left him. Then Amnon said to Tamar, "Bring the food here into my bedroom so I may eat from your hand." And Tamar took the bread she had prepared and brought it to her brother Amnon in his bedroom.

But when she took it to him to eat, he grabbed her and said, "Come to bed with me, my sister." "No, my brother!" she said to him. "Don't force me! Such a thing should not be done in Israel! Don't do this wicked thing. What about me? Where could I get rid of my disgrace? And what about you? You would be like one of the wicked fools in Israel. Please speak to the king; he will not keep me from being married to you." But he refused to listen to her, and since he was stronger than she, he raped her.

Then Amnon hated her with intense hatred. In fact, he hated her more than he had loved her. Amnon said to her, "Get up and get out!" "No!" she said to him. "Sending me away would be a greater wrong than what you have already done to me." But he refused to listen to her. He called his personal servant and said, "Get this woman out of my sight and bolt the door after her." So, his servant put her out and bolted the door after her. She was wearing an ornate robe, for this was the kind of garment the virgin daughters of the king wore. Tamar put ashes on her head and tore the ornate robe she was wearing.

She put her hands on her head and went away, weeping aloud as she went. Her brother Absalom said to her, "Has that Amnon, your brother, been with you? Be quiet for now, my sister; he is your brother. Don't take this thing to heart." And Tamar lived in her brother Absalom's house, a desolate woman. When King David heard all this, he was furious. And Absalom never said a word to Amnon, either good or bad; he hated Amnon because he had disgraced his sister Tamar (2 Samuel 13:1–22, NIV).

Amnon's abuse of his half-sister is an evil act that is way beyond anything that most of us with healthy sibling relationships can comprehend. The very last place that a younger sister like Tamar would have thought that she would be in any danger would have been at her own brother's house. In healthy families, brothers tend to be very protective of their sisters, whether they're younger or older. Tamar was fully at ease in Amnon's house, and due to her youth and naivety, she missed all the danger signs. This poor young woman's life was irreversibly damaged. When Tamar's older brother with whom she shared the same mum, Absalom, learned about what had happened, he was so enraged that he wanted to kill Amnon. Instead of doing so right away, he temporarily covered up his anger, and secretly came up with a way to avenge his sister's disgrace. But when King David learned about his beautiful young daughter's traumatic experience, he did absolutely nothing.

> *Do you think David's lack of action was because of his own sense of guilt about his poor example? Or perhaps he felt that he lacked the moral credibility to punish Amnon?*

Whatever his reasons were for doing nothing, King David had denied Tamar the justice that she deserved, both as his daughter and a citizen of his realm after being the victim of such a vile crime. As their father and the king, ensuring that justice was fully served and guilty parties were punished was part of his duties. But as we just learned, after hearing about this awful incident, David took no action at all. He did not have Amnon arrested or punished, neither did he enforce justice on Tamar's behalf. And because David did nothing to ensure that justice was carried out, as time went on, Absalom became more enraged and bitter so that he finally resolved to take matters into his own hands. The opportunity to comfort Tamar and restore her dignity within their community had been lost. King David had, unfortunately for everyone, made another extremely poor life choice. Sometime later, Absalom's evil plot to avenge his sister led to another horrific incident in David's family life; a direct *consequence* of his hiding from the horrible truth instead of handling it correctly, as he was love and duty bound.

Two years later, when Absalom's sheepshearers were at Baal Hazor near the border of Ephraim, he invited all the king's sons to come there. Absalom went to the king and said, "Your servant has had shearers come. Will the king and his attendants please join me?" "No, my son," the king replied. "All of us should not go; we would only be a burden to you." Although Absalom urged him, he still refused to go but gave him his blessing. Then Absalom said, "If not, please let my brother Amnon come with us." The king asked him, "Why should he go with you?" But Absalom urged him, so he sent with him Amnon and the rest of the king's sons.

Absalom ordered his men, "Listen! When Amnon is in high spirits from drinking wine and I say to you, 'Strike Amnon down,' then kill him. Don't be afraid. Haven't I given you this order? Be strong and brave." So Absalom's men did to Amnon what Absalom had ordered. Then all the king's sons got up, mounted their mules and fled. While they were on their way, the report came to David: "Absalom has struck down all the king's sons; not one of them is left." The king stood up, tore his clothes and lay down on the ground; and all his attendants stood by with their clothes torn. But Jonadab son of Shimeah, David's brother, said, "My lord should not think that they killed all the princes; only Amnon is dead. This has been Absalom's express intention ever since the day Amnon raped his sister Tamar. My lord the king should not be concerned about the report that all the king's sons are dead. Only Amnon is dead" (2 Samuel 13:23–33, NIV).

David would again mourn the death of another one of his children, Amnon. The fallout from all these tragic events would later also have a spillover effect on his entire nation. Although, as I have previously stated, King David was a great leader in many ways, he was a woeful parent. But this very flawed man would again have to show all of us how to reignite our momentum after failing.

> David mourned many days for his son Amnon. Absalom fled to his grandfather, Talmai son of Ammihud, the king of Geshur. He stayed there in Geshur for three years. And King David, now reconciled to Amnon's death, longed to be reunited with his son Absalom (2 Samuel 13:37, NLT).

> Then Joab went to Geshur and brought Absalom back to Jerusalem. But the king gave this order: "Absalom may go to his own house, but he must never come into my presence." So,

Absalom did not see the king. Absalom lived in Jerusalem for two years, but he never got to see the king. Then Absalom sent for Joab to ask him to intercede for him, but Joab refused to come. Absalom sent for him a second time, but again Joab refused to come. So, Absalom said to his servants, "Go and set fire to Joab's barley field, the field next to mine." So, they set his field on fire, as Absalom had commanded. Then Joab came to Absalom at his house and demanded, "Why did your servants set my field on fire?" And Absalom replied, "Because I wanted you to ask the king why he brought me back from Geshur if he didn't intend to see me. I might as well have stayed there. Let me see the king; if he finds me guilty of anything, then let him kill me." So, Joab told the king what Absalom had said. Then at last David summoned Absalom, who came and bowed low before the king, and the king kissed him (2 Samuel 14:23–24, 28–33, NLT).

Reconciling with his son Absalom after he had murdered his half-brother and restoring him back to his original position as a prince of the realm was exactly what God had previously done for King David after his sins against Bathsheba and Uriah. Forgiveness and grace on God's part had allowed David to remain in his position as the

King. So, this grieving father chose to do the same for his son. David chose to get unstuck from this terrible situation and reignite his momentum by forgiving his son. He again moved his and his family's lives forward in the positive direction. The takeaway from all of these is

> *We cannot undo the past. So, all that we*
> *can do is release it, and push forward*
> *in any positive ways that we can.*

David once again teaches us not to remain in the valley of despair or continue to beat ourselves up with guilt over our past poor choices, but instead, to trust in God again for His forgiveness, mercy, love, and grace.

> O Israel, hope in the LORD; for with the LORD there is unfailing love. His redemption overflows, (Psalm 130:7, NLT).

Reconciling with Absalom after he had wreaked such havoc in their family must have been extremely difficult for King David. After Absalom's return, the very first meeting that they had to clear the air between them must have been the most difficult. Because it was a heart-wrenching set of circumstances. But I must share my observations at this point: Even though King David had handled this situation extremely poorly, Absalom had still displayed some very troubling behavior when he returned back to

Jerusalem. This would later create a fresh crop of disasters for his father King David and their country. But in the meantime, the father and son held the toughest conversation that they had ever had and reunited. This ended the stalemate. It was the only way forward to restore their family ties. A word of caution here, however: It might not always be possible for people to reconcile with the person or persons with whom they are at odds. This is because others might not be willing or able to participate with us in a process of forgiveness and reconciliation, for too many reasons to explore in this discussion. But these two men set aside their differences, pushed past their hatred and grief, and reignited momentum.

> *In what healthy ways can a person respond to tragedy?*

I pray for all of us that we will receive the strength from God to get past any past traumas that we might have experienced so that we may also get to a point in the future where we are able to help others who are suffering as we once were and bringing comfort and hope to them.

> The Spirit of the Sovereign LORD is on me, because the LORD has anointed me to proclaim good news to the poor. He has sent me to *bind up the brokenhearted*, to proclaim freedom for the captives and release from darkness for the

prisoners, to proclaim the year of the LORD's favor and the day of vengeance of our God, to comfort all who mourn (Isaiah 61:1–2, NIV; emphasis added).

As a mother comforts her child, so will I comfort you; and you will be comforted (Isaiah 66:13, NIV).

Comfort, comfort my people, says your God (Isaiah 40:1, NIV).

God's inclusion of both the ugly and lovely parts of human history is a great testament to the veracity of His word. If He had just wanted to paint an idyllic picture of his creation, the Bible would have been a very different book. God recorded all these incidents for us so that we can learn from one another's mistakes, avoiding and correcting them in our own lives. We also get to learn about God's love, forgiveness, and grace. He had completely forgiven David for all of his sins, and granted him the grace to overcome all the ugly consequences. God sent His only begotten son, Jesus Christ, to pay for all our sins on the cross. It is vital for all of us that we take full advantage of our Savior's sacrifice before leaving the planet. We must also share this good news with as many people as we can!

When Adam sinned, sin entered the world. Adam's sin brought death, so death spread to everyone, for everyone sinned. But there is a great difference between Adam's sin and God's gracious gift. For the sin of this one man, Adam, brought death to many. But even greater is God's wonderful grace and his gift of forgiveness to many through this other man, Jesus Christ. And the result of God's gracious gift is very different from the result of that one man's sin. For Adam's sin led to condemnation, but God's free gift leads to our being made right with God, even though we are guilty of many sins. For the sin of this one man, Adam, caused death to rule over many. But even greater is God's wonderful grace and his gift of righteousness, for all who receive it will live in triumph over sin and death through this one man, Jesus Christ. Yes, Adam's one sin brings condemnation for everyone, but Christ's one act of righteousness brings a right relationship with God and new life for everyone (Romans 5:12, 15–18, NLT).

But how can they call on him to save them unless they believe in him? And how can they believe in him if they have never heard about him? And how can they hear about him unless someone tells them? And how will anyone go and tell them without being sent? That is why the Scriptures say, "How beautiful are the feet of messengers who bring good news!" (Romans 10:14–15, NLT).

Some powerfully redemptive words written by Julia H. Johnston, a Presbyterian pastor's daughter from Ohio, spring to my mind at this point. They capture the depth, wealth, and greatness of God's mercy when He rescues us.

> Marvelous grace of our loving Lord,
> Grace that exceeds our sin and our guilt!
> Yonder on Calvary's mount outpoured,
> there where the blood of the Lamb was spilt.
> Grace, grace, God's grace,
> Grace that will pardon and cleanse within;
> Grace, grace, God's grace,
> Grace that is greater than all our sin.
> Sin and despair, like the sea waves cold,
> Threaten the soul with infinite loss;
> Grace that is greater, yes, grace untold,
> Points to the Refuge, the Mighty Cross.
> Grace, grace, God's grace,
> Grace that will pardon and cleanse within;
> Grace, grace, God's grace,
> Grace that is greater than all our sin.

Are you willing to receive God's grace to push past your own difficulties, especially if confronted by the unforeseen consequences of your previous wrongdoings?

Chapter Nine

More Is Caught than Taught

As parents, we must be extremely cautious about the examples that we set for our children, because when it comes to raising children, more is caught than taught. As we just learned, after Amnon's death, David completely forgave Absalom and pressed on. This could only have been done by God's grace, because parents who have lost a child tell how extremely difficult it is to move on after such a devastating loss. This level of trauma takes a lifetime to grieve, and each person does this in their own way. Casting ourselves entirely on God's grace, reaching out for help, and finding positive coping skills to overcome grief are all essential ways to forcefully advance toward recovery. Whenever things are not within our control, we need to do our best to release them, focusing instead on those things that we can still act upon.

King David would, however, need more grace from God to navigate another set of circumstances that were also a part of the consequences of his sins. The next boulder that hit him was when his son, Absalom, began to lust for his father's power. He appeared to still hold a grudge against his dad despite their earlier reconciliation. The bitterness in Absalom's heart and his contempt for his father grew and became so strong that he finally decided to overthrow David and usurp the throne. A series of heart-breaking events would follow that negatively impacted King David's family and nation.

> After this, Absalom bought a chariot and horses, and he hired fifty bodyguards to run ahead of him. He got up early every morning and went out to the gate of the city. When people brought a case to the king for judgment, Absalom would ask where in Israel they were from, and they would tell him their tribe. Then Absalom would say, "You've really got a strong case here! It's too bad the king doesn't have anyone to hear it. I wish I were the judge. Then everyone could bring their cases to me for judgment, and I would give them justice!" When people tried to bow before him, Absalom wouldn't let them. Instead, he took them by the hand and kissed them. Absalom did this with everyone who came to the king for judgment, and so he stole the hearts of all the people of Israel.
> After four years, Absalom said to the king, "Let me go to Hebron to offer a sacrifice to the Lord and fulfill a vow I made to him. For

while your servant was at Geshur in Aram, I promised to sacrifice to the Lord in Hebron if he would bring me back to Jerusalem." "All right," the king told him. "Go and fulfill your vow." So Absalom went to Hebron. But while he was there, he sent secret messengers to all the tribes of Israel to stir up a rebellion against the king. "As soon as you hear the ram's horn," his message read, "you are to say, 'Absalom has been crowned king in Hebron.'" He took 200 men from Jerusalem with him as guests, but they knew nothing of his intentions. While Absalom was offering the sacrifices, he sent for Ahithophel, one of David's counselors who lived in Giloh. Soon many others also joined Absalom, and the conspiracy gained *momentum*

A messenger soon arrived in Jerusalem to tell David, "All Israel has joined Absalom in a conspiracy against you!" "Then we must flee at once, or it will be too late!" David urged his men. "Hurry! If we get out of the city before Absalom arrives, both we and the city of Jerusalem will be spared from disaster." "We are with you," his advisers replied. "Do what you think is best." So the king and all his household set out at once. He left no one behind except ten of his concubines to look after the palace (2 Samuel 15:1–16, NLT; emphasis added).

Meanwhile, Absalom and all the army of Israel arrived at Jerusalem, accompanied by Ahithophel. When David's friend Hushai the Arkite arrived, he went immediately to see Absalom. "Long live the king!" he exclaimed. "Long live the king!" "Is this the way you treat your friend David?" Absalom asked him. "Why aren't you with him?" "I'm here because I belong to the man who is chosen by the Lord and by all the men of Israel," Hushai replied. "And anyway, why shouldn't I serve you? Just as I was your father's adviser, now I will be your adviser!" Then Absalom turned to Ahithophel and asked him, "What should I do next?" Ahithophel told him, "Go and sleep with your father's concubines, for he has left them here to look after the palace. Then all Israel will know that you have insulted your father beyond hope of reconciliation, and they will throw their support to you."

So, they set up a tent on the palace roof where everyone could see it, and Absalom went in and had sex with his father's concubines.

Absalom followed Ahithophel's advice, just as David had done. For every word Ahithophel spoke seemed as wise as though it had come directly from the mouth of God (2 Samuel 16:15–23, NLT; emphasis added).

Do you recall the following words spoken by the Prophet Nathan regarding all of this?

> This is what the Lord says: Because of what you have done, I will cause your own household to rebel against you. I will give your wives to another man before your very eyes, and he will go to bed with them in public view. You did it secretly, but I will make this happen to you openly in the sight of all Israel (2 Samuel 12:11, NLT).

After violating another man's marital bed, David would witness his own son openly do the same to him. This is all so sad. I feel so sorry for Bathsheba and all of the innocent women who were caught up in this mess, and who had to suffer greatly because of other people's sinful choices. They were powerless to do anything against the sovereign because all the power was on King David's side. All the evil consequences of King David's sins were ugly in all regards. Later on in our discussion, I will be touching on how God's grace applies to all of these women as well as King David. But all praises again go to God! Because in the midst of these tragedies, the following promise from God's word proved to be true.

> But as people sinned more and more, God's wonderful grace became more abundant (Romans 5:20, NLT).

King David would again experience the riches of God's grace and show all of us the way out of our most horrible mistakes. Even in the midst of this most horrific set of circumstances, he reapplied the powerful principle of momentum and moved things forward as he had done before. He began by again seeking God, and yielding himself completely to His grace. The very first thing that King David did after Absalom's revolt was to preserve his own life. Because as the saying by Roman orator Cicero goes: "While there's life, there's hope."

Secondly, he secured the lives of the innocent citizens in his country by fleeing from Jerusalem, taking only his most trusted aides with him. This prevented fierce fighting from breaking out between the two factions in their capital city and other parts of the nation. Although King David repeatedly failed woefully as a parent, as a leader he has so much to teach all of us about navigating through our greatest mistakes and ending up on the victorious side.

> The king and all his people set out on foot, pausing at the last house to let all the king's men move past to lead the way. There were 600 men from Gath who had come with David, along with the king's bodyguard.
>
> Then the king turned and said to Ittai, a leader of the men from Gath, "Why are you coming with us? Go on back to King Absalom,

for you are a guest in Israel, a foreigner in exile. You arrived only recently, and should I force you today to wander with us? I don't even know where we will go. Go on back and take your kinsmen with you, and may the Lord show you his unfailing love and faithfulness." But Ittai said to the king, "I vow by the Lord and by your own life that I will go wherever my lord the king goes, no matter what happens—whether it means life or death." David replied, "All right, come with us." So Ittai and all his men and their families went along. Everyone cried loudly as the king and his followers passed by. They crossed the Kidron Valley and then went out toward the wilderness. Zadok and all the Levites also came along, carrying the Ark of the Covenant of God. They set down the Ark of God, and Abiathar offered sacrifices until everyone had passed out of the city. Then the king instructed Zadok to take the Ark of God back into the city. "If the Lord sees fit," David said, "he will bring me back to see the Ark and the Tabernacle again. But if he is through with me, then let him do what seems best to him" (2 Samuel 15:17–26, NLT).

Despite having committed the most egregious of sins, after repenting David again began the process of recovery by reconnecting with God and casting himself entirely on His mercy. Then he took all the actions that were necessary to put a halt to Absalom's momentum. David also secretly sent some of his most trustworthy servants back to the palace, planting them amongst Absalom's advisers to thwart any good advice that his son might receive. This brilliant strategy proved crucial to David's successful return to the throne. It helped to turn Absalom away from the brilliant advice offered to him by a man who had previously been David's chief adviser, Ahithophel.

> "Now in those days the advice Ahithophel gave was like that of one who inquires of God. That was how both David and Absalom regarded all of Ahithophel's advice" (2 Samuel 16:23, NIV). For reasons unknown to us, this brilliant man, who had once been so loyal to King David, became a part of Absalom's rebellion.
>
> David walked up the road to the Mount of Olives, weeping as he went. His head was covered and his feet were bare as a sign of mourning. And the people who were with him covered their heads and wept as they climbed the hill. When someone told David that his adviser Ahithophel was now backing Absalom, David prayed, "O LORD, let Ahithophel give Absalom foolish advice!" When David reached the summit of the Mount of Olives where people

worshiped God, Hushai the Arkite was waiting there for him. Hushai had torn his clothing and put dirt on his head as a sign of mourning. But David told him, "If you go with me, you will only be a burden. Return to Jerusalem and tell Absalom, 'I will now be your adviser, O king, just as I was your father's adviser in the past.' Then you can frustrate and counter Ahithophel's advice. Zadok and Abiathar, the priests, will be there. Tell them about the plans being made in the king's palace, and they will send their sons Ahimaaz and Jonathan to tell me what is going on." So David's friend Hushai returned to Jerusalem, getting there just as Absalom arrived (2 Samuel 15:30–37, NLT; see also 2 Samuel 17).

The next action that David took to reignite his momentum was by far the most difficult one of all. He went to battle against his own son. This was unavoidable at that point in order for him to regain the throne that God had given to him. David went out to battle against Absalom. Even though he did not know exactly how things would turn out, he simply trusted in God, and as previously mentioned,

> *On our knees in prayers to God is the best way to begin to reignite our momentum.*

After seeking God, we must take whatever actions are necessary, just as David did.

> David now mustered the men who were with him and appointed generals and captains to lead them. He sent the troops out in three groups, placing one group under Joab, one under Joab's brother Abishai son of Zeruiah, and one under Ittai, the man from Gath. The king told his troops, "I am going out with you." But his men objected strongly. "You must not go," they urged. "If we have to turn and run—and even if half of us die—it will make no difference to Absalom's troops; they will be looking only for you. You are worth 10,000 of us, and it is better that you stay here in the town and send help if we need it."
>
> "If you think that's the best plan, I'll do it," the king answered. So he stood alongside the gate of the town as all the troops marched out in groups of hundreds and of thousands. And the king gave this command to Joab, Abishai, and Ittai: "For my sake, deal gently with young Absalom." And all the troops heard the king give this order to his commanders. So the battle began in the forest of Ephraim, and the Israelite troops were beaten back by David's men. There was a great slaughter that day, and 20,000 men laid down their lives.

The battle raged all across the countryside, and more men died because of the forest than were killed by the sword. During the battle, Absalom happened to come upon some of David's men. He tried to escape on his mule, but as he rode beneath the thick branches of a great tree, his hair got caught in the tree. His mule kept going and left him dangling in the air. One of David's men saw what had happened and told Joab, "I saw Absalom dangling from a great tree." "What?" Joab demanded. "You saw him there and didn't kill him? I would have rewarded you with ten pieces of silver and a hero's belt!" "I would not kill the king's son for even a thousand pieces of silver," the man replied to Joab. "We all heard the king say to you and Abishai and Ittai, 'For my sake, please spare young Absalom.' And if I had betrayed the king by killing his son—and the king would certainly find out who did it—you yourself would be the first to abandon me." "Enough of this nonsense," Joab said. Then he took three daggers and plunged them into Absalom's heart as he dangled, still alive, in the great tree. Ten of Joab's young armor bearers then surrounded Absalom and killed him. Then Joab blew the ram's horn, and his men returned from chasing the army of Israel. They threw Absalom's body into a deep pit in the forest and piled a great heap of stones over it. And all Israel fled to their homes (2 Samuel 18:1–17, NLT).

Then the man from Ethiopia arrived and said, "I have good news for my lord the king. Today the Lord has rescued you from all those who rebelled against you." "What about young Absalom?" the king demanded.

"Is he all right?" And the Ethiopian replied, "May all of your enemies, my lord the king, both now and in the future, share the fate of that young man!" The king was overcome with emotion. He went up to the room over the gateway and burst into tears. And as he went, he cried, "O my son Absalom! My son, my son Absalom! If only I had died instead of you! O Absalom, my son, my son" (2 Samuel 18:31–33, NLT).

Another word of caution at this point is this: The immeasurable riches of God's grace that we see being granted to King David in no way means that we should intentionally go on sinning, because that would be contemptuous toward God, and be an abuse of His abundant mercies.

Or do you have no regard for the wealth of His kindness and tolerance and patience [in withholding His wrath]? Are you [actually] unaware or ignorant [of the fact] that God's kindness leads you to repentance [that is, to change your inner self, your old way of thinking—seek His purpose for your life]? (Romans 2:4, AMP; brackets in the original).

From all that we've learned so far, we know that because God has granted human beings free will and the freedom to choose between right and wrong, He will not always prevent us from making the wrong choices. But He gets to have the final say on what the consequences of all our choices will be. An example of this can be seen in his counsel to the nation of Israel. See Deuteronomy 30:11–20, see also Genesis 2:16–17.

After winning the battle against Absalom, "when David came to his palace in Jerusalem, he took the ten concubines he had left to look after the palace and placed them in seclusion. Their needs were provided for, but he no longer slept with them. So, each of them lived like a widow until she died" (2 Samuel 20:3, NLT). As mentioned earlier, this was so terribly sad for all these women. They had unfortunately found themselves caught up in a horrendous power struggle between their family members. All these sad consequences were a direct result of David's disobedience to God. Firstly, the King of Israel was also not supposed to have multiple wives (see Deuteronomy 17:17). Secondly, he committed adultery and murder. Had David not violated

Uriah's marriage, none of these horrific things would have happened.

> You must not commit adultery (Exodus 20:14, NLT).

> Do not defile yourself by having sexual intercourse with your neighbor's wife (Leviticus 18:20, NLT).

David's son, Absalom, had also violated God's commands by choosing to dishonor his father in the vilest ways possible.

> Honor your father and mother. Then you will live a long, full life in the land the LORD your God is giving you (Exodus 20:12, NLT).

> Honor your father and mother. This is the first commandment with a promise (Ephesians 6:2, NLT).

> *I've often wondered if King David could have avoided this entire nightmare if he had lovingly disciplined his son earlier on in his life.*

But when Absalom began to lust for his father's throne, just as he had done in Amnon's case, his father King

David did absolutely nothing, either as a parent or Israel's leader, to stop him. David's failures as a parent led to both personal and national tragedies. But again, thanks be to God! Although He does not always remove all our negative consequences, He does completely forgive and wipe away our sins when we repent. Then He promises to work all things together for our good and His glory. The sacrifice of God's only begotten son, Jesus Christ, on the cross for human beings' sins, delivers all those who will receive God's free pardon from their sins and their evil consequences.

> Even though we were dead because of our sins, he gave us life when he raised Christ from the dead. *(It is only by God's grace that you have been saved!)* For he raised us from the dead along with Christ and seated us with him in the heavenly realms because we are united with Christ Jesus. So, God can point to us in all future ages as examples of the incredible wealth of his grace and kindness toward us, as shown in all he has done for us who are united with Christ Jesus (Ephesians 2:5–7, NLT; emphasis added).

God alone determines what the just punishment for our violations of His commands will be. Because He is the righteous judge of the whole earth.

> The LORD is king! Let the earth rejoice! Let the farthest coastlands be glad … Righteousness and justice are the foundation of his throne (Psalm 97:1–2, NLT).

After King David's full and feeling repentance, God forgave all his sins and preserved his life, allowing him to continue as Israel's King. He gave David complete victory over his son's revolt. The nation of Israel, through King David's family line, would be the one through whom the Messiah and Savior of the whole world, Jesus Christ, God's only begotten son, would be born.

Mercifully, God did not allow King David to die at the hand of his own son.

God promises to forgive all our sins too, if we repent from them.

> Yet he was merciful; he forgave their iniquities and did not destroy them. Time after time he restrained his anger and did not stir up his full wrath (Psalm 78:38, NIV).

> Because I, the LORD, do not change, you descendants of Jacob have not been destroyed (Malachi 3:6, Berean Standard Bible).

With regard to Bathsheba, Tamar, and all the ladies whom Absalom publicly violated, we must have faith in God. The same grace that God made available to King David was available to them. Their lives were just as precious to God as King David's was. Innocent lives sometimes get caught up in the crossfires of other people's wrongdoings. But we must let God do our avenging, and not seek revenge for any wrongdoings done to us by others. Because if we choose to avenge ourselves, we might end up hurting many more innocent lives than we could ever imagine.

> Do not take revenge, my dear friends, but leave room for God's wrath, for it is written: "It is mine to avenge; I will repay," says the Lord (Romans 12:19, NIV).

> Let them sing before the LORD, for he comes to judge the earth. He will judge the world in righteousness and the peoples with equity (Psalm 98:9, NIV).

Jesus Christ, God's only begotten son, and many of God's faithful servants were also unjustly convicted of crimes that they did not commit, and were cruelly punished and murdered (see Matthew 23:34–35; Acts 8:2–3). For ever since our original parents, Adam and Eve, rebelled against God in the Garden of Eden, suffering from the wrongdoings done by others has become a sad reality in our human experience. Their rebellion has brought so much suffering and death to all human beings. But God promises to avenge all the injustices that take place on our planet and, ultimately, work everything together for the good of all those who love Him. This answer may not entirely satisfy those of us who may have already experienced the worst sort of traumas in life, but I pray that the following verses will reassure you of God's love and His commitment to justice's being served.

> The Lord is a God who avenges.
>   O God who avenges, shine forth.
> Rise up, Judge of the earth;
>   pay back to the proud what they deserve.
> How long, Lord, will the wicked,
>   how long will the wicked be jubilant?
> They pour out arrogant words;
>   all the evildoers are full of boasting.
> They crush your people, Lord;
>   they oppress your inheritance.
> They slay the widow and the foreigner;
>   they murder the fatherless.
> They say, "The Lord does not see;
>   the God of Jacob takes no notice."
> Take notice, you senseless ones among the people;
>   you fools, when will you become wise?

Does he who fashioned the ear not hear?
Does he who formed the eye not see?
Does he who disciplines nations not punish?
Does he who teaches mankind lack knowledge?
The Lord knows all human plans;
    he knows that they are futile.
Blessed is the one you discipline, Lord,
    the one you teach from your law;
    you grant them relief from days of trouble,
    till a pit is dug for the wicked.
For the Lord will not reject his people;
    he will never forsake his inheritance.
Judgment will again be founded on righteousness,
    and all the upright in heart will follow it.
Who will rise up for me against the wicked?
Who will take a stand for me against evildoers?
Unless the Lord had given me help,
I would soon have dwelt in the silence of death.
When I said, "My foot is slipping,"
    your unfailing love, Lord, supported me.
When anxiety was great within me,
    your consolation brought me joy.
Can a corrupt throne be allied with you—
    a throne that brings on misery by its decrees?
The wicked band together against the righteous
    and condemn the innocent to death.
But the Lord has become my fortress,

> and my God the rock in whom I take refuge.
> He will repay them for their sins
> > and destroy them for their wickedness;
> > the Lord our God will destroy them
>
> (Psalm 94:1–23, NIV).

> *Those who find themselves powerless against evil governments, people, or institutions in this world, will one day have the justice that they deserve meted out by God on their behalf, whether here, on the earth, or in eternity.*

Many people who did not receive justice here on earth will without doubt receive eternal comfort, blessings, and rewards that are uniquely designed for them by God. Please do not give up. God's truth and justice will ultimately prevail. We're given another glimpse of this in the following example.

> There was a rich man who was dressed in purple and fine linen and lived in luxury every day. At his gate was laid a beggar named Lazarus, covered with sores and longing to eat what fell from the rich man's table. Even the dogs came and licked his sores. "The time came when the beggar died and the angels carried him to Abraham's side. The rich man also died and was buried. In Hades, where he was in torment, he looked up

> and saw Abraham far away, with Lazarus by his side. So, he called to him, "Father Abraham, have pity on me and send Lazarus to dip the tip of his finger in water and cool my tongue, because I am in agony in this fire." But Abraham replied, "Son, remember that in your lifetime you received your good things, while Lazarus received bad things, but now he is comforted here and you are in agony. And besides all this, between us and you a great chasm has been set in place, so that those who want to go from here to you cannot, nor can anyone cross over from there to us" (Luke 16:19–26, NIV; see also Hebrews 11:13–16, 35–40, 12:1–3).

Jesus also told his disciples the following very difficult truths that are great challenges to our faith. "But I tell you, do not resist an evil person. If anyone slaps you on the right cheek, turn to them the other cheek also" (Matthew 5:39, NIV).

> You have heard that it was said, "Love your neighbor and hate your enemy." But I tell you, love your enemies and pray for those who persecute you, that you may be children of your Father in heaven. He causes his sun to rise on the evil and the good, and sends rain on the righteous and the unrighteous. If you love those

who love you, what reward will you get? (Matthew 5:43–46, NIV).

Maintaining the love position in our hearts, when hatred and revenge feel the most right, requires nothing less than placing our complete faith in God, and receiving the grace from Him to submit our hearts to His commands.

There were times in the Bible, however, when God directly intervened to correct man's inhumanity toward one another. On one such occasion, a young woman by the name of Leah—who was most likely a teenager, because most women were married off at very young ages during her times—was persuaded by her evil father, Laban, to join in a scheme to deceive a young man named Jacob into marrying her. The only problem was that Jacob was clearly in love with her more beautiful younger sister, Rachel, and was pledged to marry her after working for their father for seven years. But Laban chose to enrich himself at the expense of his two daughters' happiness. And by the way, Laban was also Jacob's uncle. Here is how it happened:

> Now Laban had two daughters. The older daughter was named Leah, and the younger one was Rachel. There was no sparkle in Leah's eyes, but Rachel had a beautiful figure and a lovely

face. Since Jacob was in love with Rachel, he told her father, "I'll work for you for seven years if you'll give me Rachel, your younger daughter, as my wife." "Agreed!" Laban replied. "I'd rather give her to you than to anyone else. Stay and work with me." So Jacob worked seven years to pay for Rachel. But his love for her was so strong that it seemed to him but a few days. Finally, the time came for him to marry her. "I have fulfilled my agreement," Jacob said to Laban. "Now give me my wife so I can sleep with her." So Laban invited everyone in the neighborhood and prepared a wedding feast. But that night, when it was dark, Laban took Leah to Jacob, and he slept with her. (Laban had given Leah a servant, Zilpah, to be her maid.) But when Jacob woke up in the morning—it was Leah! "What have you done to me?" Jacob raged at Laban. "I worked seven years for Rachel! Why have you tricked me?"

"It's not our custom here to marry off a younger daughter ahead of the firstborn," Laban replied. "But wait until the bridal week is over; then we'll give you Rachel, too—provided you promise to work another seven years for me." So Jacob agreed to work seven more years. A week after Jacob had married Leah, Laban gave him Rachel, too. (Laban gave Rachel a servant,

> Bilhah, to be her maid.) So Jacob slept with Rachel, too, and he loved her much more than Leah. He then stayed and worked for Laban the additional seven years (Genesis 29: 16–30, NLT).

Leah had probably been belittled and made to feel as if she could never get a spouse on her own because of her less attractive physical appearance. And being so young and insecure, she was probably easily coerced by her greedy dad. Because women had less freedom in their lives and marriages during those times, they had to follow the path that was laid out for them. Understandably, after this terrible trick that was played on him, Jacob hated Leah and treated her very poorly. But God decided to directly intervene to help her.

> When the Lord saw that Leah was unloved, he enabled her to have children, but Rachel could not conceive. So, Leah became pregnant and gave birth to a son. She named him Reuben, for she said, "The Lord has noticed my misery, and now my husband will love me." She soon became pregnant again and gave birth to another son. She named him Simeon, for she said, "The Lord heard that I was unloved and has given me another son." Then she became pregnant a third time and gave birth to another son. He

was named Levi, for she said, "Surely this time my husband will feel affection for me, since I have given him three sons!" Once again Leah became pregnant and gave birth to another son. She named him Judah, for she said, "Now I will praise the Lord!" And then she stopped having children (Genesis 29: 31–35, NLT; emphasis added).

> *Beautiful timing and making things right for people in His own righteous way is entirely God's call.*

He is the only one in possession of all the truth relating to any and every matter. All these poor women and others in terrible situations must be assured that God will forgive, heal, and avenge us. He is the only one with the power to redeem our pasts. "The LORD says, 'I will give you back what you lost'" (Joel 2:25, NLT). "I will save you" (Ezekiel 36:29, NIV). The right response on our part is always to take ownership of and genuinely repent of our own sins. This mends our broken relationship with God. But King David fully regained his *momentum* and went on to complete his term as the King of Israel. Then he passed on his throne to the second son that he and Bathsheba had, Solomon, who as mentioned earlier became one of the wealthiest kings in human history, Shedding great glory on his father King David's name. The whole situation with Absalom really does give all of us a lot to think about, doesn't it? It is an excruciatingly painful illustration of the following scripture verse: A man's enemies will be the members of his own household (Matthew 10:36, NIV).

God's mercy is available to anyone who calls upon him. Not only for Kings or rulers like David.

> Everyone who calls on the name of the LORD will be saved (Romans 10:13, NLT).

> Seek the LORD while you can find him. Call on him now while he is near. Let the wicked change their ways and banish the very thought of doing wrong. Let them turn to the LORD that he may have mercy on them. Yes, turn to our God, for he will forgive generously (Isaiah 55:6–7, NLT). Amen.

Will you receive God's grace today, right now, to leave the avenging of any wrongs done to you by others to Him?

Chapter Ten

WAIT, WHAT? KING DAVID FAILS AGAIN?

King David would once again reveal his feet of clay when he violated another of God's commands. This time, it was with regard to how the Kings of Israel were to conduct national censuses. There is nothing wrong with a government wanting to know the size of its population. It's a great way for any administration to determine how goods and services are to be allocated and distributed to the people. So, periodically, governments conduct censuses. But the problem with the census that King David had conducted was that it was not done in the way that God had instructed in His laws.

> Then the LORD said to Moses, "Whenever you take a census of the people of Israel, each man who is counted must pay a ransom for himself to the LORD. Then no plague will strike the people as you count them. Each person who is counted must give a small piece of silver as a sacred offering to the LORD. (This payment is half a shekel, based on the sanctuary shekel,

which equals twenty gerahs.) All who have reached their twentieth birthday must give this sacred offering to the LORD. When this offering is given to the LORD to purify your lives, making you right with him, the rich must not give more than the specified amount, and the poor must not give less. Receive this ransom money from the Israelites, and use it for the care of the Tabernacle. It will bring the Israelites to the LORD's attention, and it will purify your lives" (Exodus 30: 11–16, NLT).

The Kings of Israel were required to know God's laws, and copy them by hand for themselves in the presence of the Levitical priests. They were to carefully read them daily for as long as they lived. Based on this, there was no excuse for David or any other King of Israel not to know what God's laws were.

When he sits on the throne as king, he must copy for himself this body of instruction on a scroll in the presence of the Levitical priests. He must always keep that copy with him and read it daily as long as he lives. That way he will learn to fear the Lord his God by obeying all the terms of these instructions and decrees. This regular reading will prevent him from becoming proud and acting as if he is above his fellow citizens. It will also prevent him from turning away from these commands in the smallest way. And it will ensure that he and his descendants will reign for many generations in Israel (Deuteronomy 17:18–20, NLT).

But King David turned a deaf ear to the advice of one of his closest advisers, deciding to do the census without following God's commands. This was a colossal error on his part, and some horrible consequences followed.

> Satan rose up against Israel and caused David to take a census of the people of Israel. So David said to Joab and the commanders of the army, "Take a census of all the people of Israel—from Beersheba in the south to Dan in the north—and bring me a report so I may know how many there are." But Joab replied, "May the Lord increase the number of his people a hundred times over! But why, my lord the king, do you want to do this? Are they not all your servants? Why must you cause Israel to sin?" But the king insisted that they take the census, so Joab traveled throughout all Israel to count the people. Then he returned to Jerusalem and reported the number of people to David. There were 1,100,000 warriors in all Israel who could handle a sword, and 470,000 in Judah. But Joab

did not include the tribes of Levi and Benjamin in the census because he was so distressed at what the king had made him do. God was very displeased with the census, and he punished Israel for it. Then David said to God, "I have sinned greatly by taking this census. Please forgive my guilt for doing this foolish thing."

Then the Lord spoke to Gad, David's seer. This was the message: "Go and say to David, 'This is what the Lord says: I will give you three choices. Choose one of these punishments, and I will inflict it on you.'" So Gad came to David and said, "These are the choices the Lord has given you. You may choose three years of famine, three months of destruction by the sword of your enemies, or three days of severe plague as the angel of the Lord brings devastation throughout the land of Israel. Decide what answer I should give the Lord who sent me." "I'm in a desperate situation!" David replied to Gad. "But let me fall into the hands of the Lord, for his mercy is very great. Do not let me fall into human hands."

So the Lord sent a plague upon Israel, and 70,000 people died as a result. And God sent an angel to destroy Jerusalem. But just as the angel was preparing to destroy it, the Lord relented and said to the death angel, "Stop! That is enough!" At that moment the angel of the Lord was standing by the threshing floor of Araunah the Jebusite. David looked up and saw the angel of the Lord standing between heaven and earth with his sword drawn, reaching out over Jerusalem. So David and the leaders of Israel put on burlap to show their deep distress and fell face down on the ground. And David said to God, "I am the one who called for the census! I am the one who has sinned and done wrong! But these people are as innocent as sheep—what have they done? O Lord my God, let your anger fall against me and my family, but do not destroy your people."

Then the angel of the Lord told Gad to instruct David to go up and build an altar to the Lord on the threshing floor of Araunah the Jebusite. So David went up to do what the Lord had commanded him through Gad. Araunah, who was busy threshing wheat at the time, turned and saw the angel there. His four sons, who were with him, ran away and hid. When Araunah saw David approaching, he left his threshing floor and bowed before David with his face to the ground. David said to Araunah, "Let me buy this threshing floor from you at its full price. Then I will build an altar to the Lord there, so that he will stop the plague." "Take it, my lord the king, and use it as you wish," Araunah said to David. "I will give the oxen for the burnt offerings, and the threshing boards for wood to build a fire on the altar, and the wheat for the grain offering. I will give it all to you." But King David replied to Araunah, "No, I insist on buying it for the full price. I will not take what is yours and give it to the Lord. I will not present burnt offerings that have cost me nothing!" So David gave Araunah 600 pieces of gold in payment for the threshing floor.

David built an altar there to the Lord and sacrificed burnt offerings and peace offerings. And when David prayed, the Lord answered him by sending fire from heaven to burn up the offering on the altar. Then the Lord spoke to the angel, who put the sword back into its sheath. When David saw that the Lord had answered his prayer, he offered sacrifices there at Araunah's threshing floor. At that time the Tabernacle of the Lord and the altar of burnt offering that Moses had made in the wilderness were located at the place of worship in Gibeon. But David was not able to go there to inquire of God, because he was terrified by the drawn sword of the angel of the Lord (1 Chronicles 21:1–30, NLT).

In another record of this same event found in 2 Samuel 24:1, we learn more about how the idea of conducting a national census entered into David's mind. "Again the anger of the LORD burned against Israel, and he incited David against them, saying, "Go and take a census of Israel and Judah" (NIV). The preceding helps us to gain more insight into why King David would choose to do something that would invoke the Lord's anger, resulting in so much loss. It was the *"anger of the LORD"* that had been stirred up against the nation of Israel. Their king was the instrument of judgment in the Lord's hands against the nation. The people had apparently severely displeased God.

The census also appears to have happened right after King David had won a major victory over the Philistines. So he might have been feeling really chuffed with himself, making him susceptible to pride (see 1 Chronicles 20). Seemingly seeking to derive some confidence from the size of Israel's army, rather than continue to draw his strength from God as he had done on previous occasions, David ignored God's clear commands. But one would have thought that after seeing the poor example that his predecessor, King Saul, had set, which had led to his downfall and removal from the throne, King David would be more cautious about following God's instructions. "But God removed Saul and replaced him with David, a man about whom God said, 'I have found David son of Jesse, a man after my own heart. He will do everything I want him to do'" (Acts 13:22, NLT).

God had said the following to Saul after he had disobeyed Him: "But now your kingdom must end, for the LORD has sought out a man after his own heart. The LORD has already appointed him to be the leader of his people, *because you have not kept the LORD's command*" (1 Samuel 13:14, NLT; emphasis added).

> *Although this was a satanic trap that had been brought on by the people's sins, as Israel's leader, King David was still responsible for the condition of his own heart and actions.*

He had clearly ignored and disobeyed God's commands on this issue. Also, note that it takes an awful lot to make such a long-suffering, loving, and compassionate God so angry that He would rise up against a nation. "The LORD is compassionate and merciful, slow to get angry and filled with unfailing love" (Psalm 103:8, NLT).

> The Lord isn't really being slow about his promise, as some people think. No, he is being patient for your sake. He does not want anyone to be destroyed, but wants everyone to repent (2 Peter 3:9, NLT).

> *This great leader would again have to show us how to ignite momentum and come out of the tragic mess that he had gotten himself and his nation into.*

As he had done on previous occasions, King David began with a genuine heartfelt repentance toward God. "Then David said to God, 'I have sinned greatly by taking this census. Please forgive my guilt for doing this foolish thing'" (1 Chronicles 21:7, NLT).

Remember that I have also cautioned earlier that we must not continue to sin just because we know that God is loving, compassionate, and merciful. This would be an abuse of His grace. But no matter how many times that we have failed, we must learn to get back up again and keep moving forward. "Well then, should we keep on sinning so that God can show us more and more of his wonderful grace? Of course not! Since we have died to sin, how can we continue to live in it? (Romans 6:1–2, NLT).

But also consider, "Don't you see how wonderfully kind, tolerant, and patient God is with you? Does this mean nothing to you? Can't you see that his kindness is intended to turn you from your sin?" (Romans 2:4, NLT).

After his heartfelt repentance toward God, David built an altar to worship Him. You might be wondering why I still consider him to be a godly man after all the wrong things that he had done. Although he was a flawed human being just as we all are, *it was David's heart for God that set him apart.*

His faith in God was deep and sincere. His humility of heart can also be seen throughout his life. He was genuine and transparent through all his struggles, and would not allow *anything*, including his own sins and failures, to stop his quest for seeking God and *successfully* fulfilling God's purpose for his life. This is why David is considered to be the standard by which all future kings of Israel and Judah were to be measured. "For though the righteous fall seven times, they rise again, but the wicked stumble when calamity strikes" (Proverbs 24:16, NIV).

> *Despite his many failures. David repeatedly repented and kept going.*

He learned how to move on from his sins and go on to accomplish God's purpose for his life. So, no matter how many times that you have failed, please do not give up. Reignite your momentum. Place your complete trust in the sacrifice that Jesus Christ made when He died on the cross for all our sins.

> For God's will was for us to be made holy by the sacrifice of the body of Jesus Christ, once for all time. Under the old covenant, the priest stands and ministers before the altar day after day, offering the same sacrifices again and again,

which can never take away sins. But our High Priest offered himself to God as a single sacrifice for sins, good for all time. Then he sat down in the place of honor at God's right hand (Hebrews 10:10–12, NLT).

He has removed our sins as far from us as the east is from the west (Psalm 103:12, NLT).

We then go on to show the fruits of our genuine repentance through our actions. King David once again reminds us that the way back from our sins is to turn back to God. Then we must continue moving forward toward fulfilling His purpose for our lives.

He is so rich in kindness and grace that he purchased our freedom with the blood of his Son and forgave our sins (Ephesians 1:7, NLT).

O Israel, hope in the LORD; for with the LORD there is unfailing love. His redemption overflows Psalm 130:7 (NLT).

When we repent from our sins, God washes them completely away as if they never had happened. Do you believe and receive this truth?

Chapter Eleven

How Do I Say This? Yep, It's David Again!

Yep, that's right. It's King David yet again! This time his failure had to do with how the Ark of the Covenant, also known as the Tabernacle of the Testimony, which represented God's presence in their nation was to be carried. King David was about to royally blow it again. Doing things in his own way rather than in God's clearly specified way.

> David again brought together all the able young men of Israel—thirty thousand. He and all his men went to Baalah in Judah to bring up from there the ark of God, which is called by the Name, the name of the Lord Almighty, who is enthroned between the cherubim on the ark. *They set the ark of God on a new cart* and brought it from the house of Abinadab, which was on the hill. Uzzah and Ahio, sons of Abinadab, were guiding the new cart with the ark of God on it, and Ahio was walking in front of it. David and all Israel were celebrating with all their might

before the Lord, with castanets, harps, lyres, timbrels, sistrums and cymbals. When they came to the threshing floor of Nakon, Uzzah reached out and took hold of the ark of God, because the oxen stumbled. The Lord's anger burned against Uzzah because of his irreverent act; therefore God struck him down, and he died there beside the ark of God. Then David was angry because the Lord's wrath had broken out against Uzzah, and to this day that place is called Perez Uzzah. David was afraid of the Lord that day and said, "How can the ark of the Lord ever come to me?" He was not willing to take the ark of the Lord to be with him in the City of David. Instead, he took it to the house of Obed-Edom the Gittite. The ark of the Lord remained in the house of Obed-Edom the Gittite for three months, and the Lord blessed him and his entire household (2 Samuel 6: 1–11, NLT).

Instead of how David chose to carry the Tabernacle of the Testimony, here is how God had instructed the Israelites to handle this most sacred object:

> But appoint the Levites over the Tabernacle of the testimony, and over all its furnishings, and over all that belongs to it. *They are to carry the Tabernacle and all its furnishings, and they shall take*

care of it and shall camp around the Tabernacle. Whenever it is time for the Tabernacle to move, the Levites will take it down. And when it is time to stop, they will set it up again. But any unauthorized person who goes too near the Tabernacle must be put to death (Numbers 1:50–51, NLT; emphasis added).

The camp will be ready to move when Aaron and his sons have finished covering the sanctuary and all the sacred articles. The Kohathites will come and carry these things to the next destination. But they must not touch the sacred objects, or they will die. So, these are the things from the Tabernacle that the Kohathites must carry (Numbers 4:15, NLT).

The Ark of the Covenant was not to be carried on a cart! Do you also recall that the Kings of Israel were supposed to write a copy of the book of God's law by hand and read it *every day*? King David must have had a copy in his possession. But do you think that he read it every day? Because if he did, he had absolutely no excuse for not knowing how God wanted things done. And if he didn't, this was a great act of disobedience that would keep landing him deep in trouble, mm-hmm. Well, I'm not sure if he had stopped reading the book of God's laws or just ignored it. But David would again learn the most tragic consequences of disobeying God's commands. So, I ask you this:

> *Do you read and meditate on God's word daily, or only when you're in trouble?*

God's believing children have been given the greatest privilege of being in His family. In our dispensation, we can come into His presence at any time without any special requirements, as we mentioned earlier. But we must never ever lose our reverence for our holy and awesome creator. "This is what the LORD said: 'I will be treated as holy by those who approach Me, and before all the people I will be honored'" (Leviticus 10:3, AMP; See also Leviticus 10:1–19).

> *We rightfully love and respect our earthly parents and those we hold in high esteem. So, what level of respect ought we to demonstrate toward the almighty God?*

Take a guess what King David did after this fatal-to-Uzzah failure. This man who had an unquenchable longing to please God, which was his reason for wanting to restore the Ark to its rightful place, once again chose to take full responsibility for his sins and repented. No excuses. But he didn't end things there. David went on to show the fruits of his genuine repentance and trust in

God's forgiveness by going right back to complete the task of bringing the Ark of God back to Jerusalem. But this time, he did things in the proper way. King David went strictly by the book and went all out in worship. No carts were allowed to be involved!

> Then King David was told, "The Lord has blessed Obededom's household and everything he has because of the Ark of God." So, David went there and brought the Ark of God from the house of Obededom to the City of David with a great celebration. *After the men who were carrying the Ark of the Lord had gone six steps, David sacrificed a bull and a fattened calf. And David danced before the Lord with all his might, wearing a priestly garment.* So David and all the people of Israel brought up the Ark of the Lord with shouts of joy and the blowing of rams' horns (2 Samuel 6: 12–15, NLT; emphasis added).

> *It is of the utmost importance to note that David not only verbally repented toward God on each occasion that he failed, but quickly followed his repentance with actions that revealed a changed heart.*

"Therefore produce fruit consistent with repentance" (Matthew 3:8, New American Standard Bible). Is this not a man in relentless pursuit of God? If this had happened to me after I had tried to do something to please and honor God, I would just have given up altogether after Uzzah died, and left God's special Ark alone, out of fear and disappointment, in both myself and God. But not King David; he once again chose to reignite his momentum by repenting of his sins, getting right back up again, and successfully completing the sacred task. King David is indeed proof to all of us that

> From six disasters he will rescue you; even in the seventh, he will keep you from evil (Job 5:19, NLT).

> The righteous person faces many troubles, but the LORD comes to the rescue each time (Psalm 34:19, NLT).

After repenting and recovering from all his failures, we learn again from King David how to stay on course. This courageous man repeatedly set things back into motion after getting stuck in sin. He just would not give up. This was why he was able to end his reign as a successful king and pass on the throne to his son, Solomon.

> Therefore produce fruit that is worthy of [and consistent with your] repentance [that is, live changed lives, turn from sin and seek God and

His righteousness]. And do not even begin to say to yourselves [as a defense], "We have Abraham for our father [and so our heritage assures us of salvation]"; for I say to you that from these stones God is able to raise up children (descendants) for Abraham [for God can replace the unrepentant, regardless of their heritage, with those who are obedient] (Luke 3:8, AMP; brackets in the original).

Amazingly, the lineage of God's only begotten son—Jesus Christ, the Savior of the whole world—is from King David's family line. Toward the end of David's life, God also made him some very powerful promises. They were beyond anything that anyone could have asked for or imagined.

> Now then, tell my servant David, "This is what the Lord Almighty says: I took you from the pasture, from tending the flock, and appointed you ruler over my people Israel. I have been with you wherever you have gone, and I have cut off all your enemies from before you. Now I will make your name great, like the names of the greatest men on earth. And I will provide a place for my people Israel and will plant them so that they can have a home of their own and no longer be disturbed. Wicked people will

not oppress them anymore, as they did at the beginning and have done ever since the time I appointed leaders over my people Israel. I will also give you rest from all your enemies. The Lord declares to you that the Lord himself will establish a house for you: When your days are over and you rest with your ancestors, I will raise up your offspring to succeed you, your own flesh and blood, and I will establish his kingdom. He is the one who will build a house for my Name, and I will establish the throne of his kingdom forever. I will be his father, and he will be my son. When he does wrong, I will punish him with a rod wielded by men, with floggings inflicted by human hands. But my love will never be taken away from him, as I took it away from Saul, whom I removed from before you. *Your house and your kingdom will endure forever before me; your throne will be established forever"* (2 Samuel 7: 8–16, NIV; emphasis added).

David responded to these unfathomably loving promises from God with more heartfelt worship.

> Then King David went in and sat before the Lord, and he said: *"Who am I, Sovereign Lord, and what is my family, that you have brought me this far?* And as if this were not enough in your

sight, Sovereign Lord, you have also spoken about the future of the house of your servant—and this decree, Sovereign Lord, is for a mere human! What more can David say to you? For you know your servant, Sovereign Lord. For the sake of your word and according to your will, you have done this great thing and made it known to your servant. How great you are, Sovereign Lord! There is no one like you, and there is no God but you, as we have heard with our own ears. And who is like your people Israel—the one nation on earth that God went out to redeem as a people for himself, and to make a name for himself, and to perform great and awesome wonders by driving out nations and their gods from before your people, whom you redeemed from Egypt? You have established your people Israel as your very own forever, and you, Lord, have become their God. And now, Lord God, keep forever the promise you have made concerning your servant and his house.

"Do as you promised, so that your name will be great forever. Then people will say, 'The Lord Almighty is God over Israel!' And the house of your servant David will be established in your sight. Lord Almighty, God of Israel, you have revealed this to your servant, saying, 'I will build a house for you.' So your servant has found courage to pray this prayer to you. Sovereign Lord, you are God! Your covenant is trustworthy, and you have promised these good things to your servant. Now be pleased to bless the house of your servant, that it may continue forever in your sight; for you, Sovereign Lord, have spoken, and with your blessing the house of your servant will be blessed forever" (2 Samuel 7: 18–29, NIV; emphasis added).

Today, the nation of Israel's flag bears the Star of David as a widely acknowledged symbol of the Jewish people. God has indeed kept all of His promises to His very flawed but faithful servant, King David. So, although you may have failed many times, please, get back up on your own feet too. God never gets weary of pardoning His children and restoring them back to His family and to His plans and purposes for their lives.

> Instead of shame and dishonor, you will enjoy a double share of honor. You will possess a double portion of prosperity in your land, and everlasting joy will be yours (Isaiah 61:7, NLT).

> But those who trust in the LORD will find new strength. They will soar high on wings like eagles. They will run and not grow weary. They will walk and not faint (Isaiah 40:31, NLT).

*Do you need more proof not to give up, but
to reignite your momentum and run on?*

Chapter Twelve

FIND FRESH STRENGTH IN GOD

I'd like to back up a bit to the period before King David took the throne as the King of Israel. At that time, he had a very fierce opponent in his predecessor, King Saul, who envied and feared David. As we learned earlier, Saul had already been rejected by God for being disobedient. His sons were also prevented from succeeding him as king after his death. When Saul had learned that David was God's choice as Israel's next leader, he waited until after the death of the prophet Samuel, who had anointed him as the first King of Israel, before embarking on his repeated attempts to kill David.

> Samuel replied, "What is more pleasing to the LORD: your burnt offerings and sacrifices or your obedience to his voice? Listen! Obedience is better than sacrifice, and submission is better than offering the fat of rams. Rebellion is as sinful as witchcraft, and stubbornness as bad as worshiping idols. *So*, because you have rejected

the command of the LORD, he has rejected you as king."

As Samuel turned to go, Saul tried to hold him back and tore the hem of his robe. And Samuel said to him, "The LORD has torn the kingdom of Israel from you today and has given it to someone else—one who is better than you" (1 Samuel 15:22–23, 27–28, NLT).

So, David fled for his life to Philistine territory to escape from King Saul. But Saul stubbornly refused to submit to God's will on this matter, and repeatedly tried to kill David. He wanted to put a permanent end to the momentum of Israel's new king, David.

But David kept thinking to himself, "Someday Saul is going to get me. The best thing I can do is escape to the Philistines. Then Saul will stop hunting for me in Israelite territory, and I will finally be safe." So David took his 600 men and went over and joined Achish son of Maoch, the king of Gath. David and his men and their families settled there with Achish at Gath. David brought his two wives along with him—Ahinoam from Jezreel and Abigail, Nabal's widow from Carmel. Word soon reached Saul that David had fled to Gath, so he stopped hunting for him. One day David said to Achish,

> "If it is all right with you, we would rather live in one of the country towns instead of here in the royal city." So Achish gave him the town of Ziklag (which still belongs to the kings of Judah to this day), and they lived there among the Philistines for a year and four months (1 Samuel 27: 1–7, NLT).

While David was living in Philistine territory in a town called Ziklag, an incident took place that would further illustrate the depth of David's dependence on God.

> When David and his men arrived home at their town of Ziklag, they found that the Amalekites had made a raid into the Negev and Ziklag; they had crushed Ziklag and burned it to the ground. They had carried off the women and children and everyone else but without killing anyone. When David and his men saw the ruins and realized what had happened to their families, they wept until they could weep no more. David's two wives, Ahinoam from Jezreel and Abigail, the widow of Nabal from Carmel, were among those captured. David was now in great danger because all his men were very bitter about losing their sons and daughters, and they began to talk of stoning him. *But David found strength in the Lord his God.* Then he said to Abiathar the priest,

"Bring me the ephod!" So Abiathar brought it. Then David asked the Lord, "Should I chase after this band of raiders? Will I catch them?" And the Lord told him, "Yes, go after them. You will surely recover everything that was taken from you!" (1 Samuel 30: 1–8, NLT; emphasis added).

> *If we learn to draw fresh strength from God no matter the circumstances, even if we have lost everything, as David did, we can still recover all and make a comeback.*

After his own followers wanted to stone him to death, David reignited his momentum again by seeking and finding fresh strength in God. After his time of worship and prayers, he took whatever actions were necessary to recover all that had been taken from him and his men.

> David and his men rushed in among them and slaughtered them throughout that night and the entire next day until evening. None of the Amalekites escaped except 400 young men who fled on camels. David got back everything the Amalekites had taken, and he rescued his two wives. Nothing was missing: small or great, son or daughter, nor anything else that had been taken. David brought everything back. He also

recovered all the flocks and herds, and his men drove them ahead of the other livestock. "This plunder belongs to David!" they said.

When he arrived at Ziklag, David sent part of the plunder to the elders of Judah, who were his friends. "Here is a present for you, taken from the Lord's enemies," he said. The gifts were sent to the people of the following towns David had visited: Bethel, Ramoth-negev, Jattir, Aroer, Siphmoth, Eshtemoa, Racal, the towns of the Jerahmeelites, the towns of the Kenites, Hormah, Bor-ashan, Athach, Hebron, and all the other places David and his men had visited (1 Samuel 30: 17–20, 26–31 NLT).

Because he continually trusted in God, the momentum was always on David's side.

"The war between the house of Saul and the house of David lasted a long time. David grew stronger and stronger, while the house of Saul grew weaker and weaker" (2 Samuel 3: 1, NIV).

David was still living in Ziklag when he finally received the news of King Saul's death. He moved to Hebron to become the king of Judah and later was crowned the king of all Israel (see 2 Samuel 1, 2:1–4, 5:1–5). So, "Saul died because he was unfaithful to the LORD; he did not keep the word of the LORD and even consulted a medium for guidance, and did not inquire of the LORD. So, the LORD put him to death and turned the kingdom over to David son of Jesse" (1 Chronicles 10:13–14, NIV). Our takeaway from this part of our discussion?

> Search for the LORD and for his strength; continually seek him (Psalm 105:4, NLT).

> I can do all things [which He has called me to do] through Him who strengthens and empowers me [to fulfill His purpose—I am self-sufficient in Christ's sufficiency; I am ready for anything and equal to anything through Him who infuses me with inner strength and confident peace] (Philippians 4:13, AMP; brackets in the original).

David continually reignited his momentum by seeking and receiving fresh strength from God. Do you regularly seek and draw your strength from God?

Chapter Thirteen

A Strong Finish from the King of Momentum!

A final word from the King of Momentum, "King David was now very old, and no matter how many blankets covered him, he could not keep warm" (1 Kings 1:1, NLT). So, another one of his sons, Adonijah, decided to take the wrong advantage of his dad's weakened state and put a final end to David's momentum. In a somewhat similar revolt to that of his brother Absalom, Adonijah tried to overturn God's will, and David's last will and testament, which stated that Solomon would be the king of Israel after David's death.

> About that time David's son Adonijah, whose mother was Haggith, began boasting, "I will make myself king." So he provided himself with chariots and charioteers and recruited fifty men to run in front of him. *Now his father, King David, had never disciplined him at any time*, even by asking, "Why are you doing that?" Adonijah had been born next after Absalom, and he was very handsome. Adonijah took Joab son of

> Zeruiah and Abiathar the priest into his confidence, and they agreed to help him become king. But Zadok the priest, Benaiah son of Jehoiada, Nathan the prophet, Shimei, Rei, and David's personal bodyguard refused to support Adonijah. Adonijah went to the Stone of Zoheleth near the spring of En-rogel, where he sacrificed sheep, cattle, and fattened calves. He invited all his brothers—the other sons of King David—and all the royal officials of Judah. But he did not invite Nathan the prophet or Benaiah or the king's bodyguard or his brother Solomon (1 Kings 1:5–10, NLT; emphasis added).

Again, we observe that King David did not discipline Adonijah as he should have done. Do you also recall that earlier on in our discussion, the Prophet Nathan had clearly told David that his son Solomon would succeed him on the throne after his death? When Nathan heard about Adonijah's plot, he moved swiftly to avert the coming disaster. They had all learned very hard lessons from Absalom's previous revolt.

> Then Nathan went to Bathsheba, Solomon's mother, and asked her, "Haven't you heard that Haggith's son, Adonijah, has made himself king, and our lord David doesn't even know about it? If you want to save your own life and

the life of your son Solomon, follow my advice. Go at once to King David and say to him, 'My lord the king, didn't you make a vow and say to me, "Your son Solomon will surely be the next king and will sit on my throne"? Why then has Adonijah become king?' And while you are still talking with him, I will come and confirm everything you have said." So Bathsheba went into the king's bedroom. (He was very old now, and Abishag was taking care of him.) Bathsheba bowed down before the king. "What can I do for you?" he asked her. She replied, "My lord, you made a vow before the Lord your God when you said to me, 'Your son Solomon will surely be the next king and will sit on my throne.' But instead, Adonijah has made himself king, and my lord the king does not even know about it. He has sacrificed many cattle, fattened calves, and sheep, and he has invited all the king's sons to attend the celebration. He also invited Abiathar the priest and Joab, the commander of the army. But he did not invite your servant Solomon. And now, my lord the king, all Israel is waiting for you to announce who will become king after you. If you do not act, my son Solomon and I will be treated as criminals as soon as my lord the king has died."

While she was still speaking with the king, Nathan the prophet arrived. The king's officials told him, "Nathan the prophet is here to see you." Nathan went in and bowed before the king with his face to the ground. Nathan asked, "My lord the king, have you decided that Adonijah will be the next king and that he will sit on your throne? Today he has sacrificed many cattle, fattened calves, and sheep, and he has invited all the king's sons to attend the celebration. He also invited the commanders of the army and Abiathar the priest. They are feasting and drinking with him and shouting, 'Long live King Adonijah!' But he did not invite me or Zadok the priest or Benaiah or your servant Solomon. Has my lord the king really done this without letting any of his officials know who should be the next king?" (1 Kings 1:11–27, NLT).

This mighty giant slayer's children had repeatedly failed to learn the lesson that despite being an extremely poor parent, King David was a powerful leader who had learned about the power that lies in seizing the momentum whenever he was stuck. This had been the key to his many successes. So, when David finally learned about his son Adonijah's attempt to usurp the throne, he strengthened himself in the Lord one final time and again seized the momentum from his rebellious child, as he had done with Absalom. King David was a devout worshiper of God, who relied completely on his relationship with God to pull through in any and every situation. Although he was quite advanced in age and very weak at this point, his spirit remained strong, and his mind sharp and clear. David knew that he must leave behind a strong legacy of faith in God's call on one's life for his family and nation.

> King David responded, "Call Bathsheba!" So she came back in and stood before the king. And the king repeated his vow: *"As surely as the Lord lives, who has rescued me from every danger, your son Solomon will be the next king and will sit on my throne this very day, just as I vowed to you before the Lord, the God of Israel."* Then Bathsheba bowed down with her face to the ground before the king and exclaimed, "May my lord King David live forever!" Then King David ordered, "Call Zadok the priest, Nathan the prophet, and Benaiah son of Jehoiada." When they came into the king's presence, the king said to them, "Take Solomon and my officials down to Gihon Spring. Solomon is to ride on my own mule. There Zadok the priest and Nathan the prophet are to anoint him king over Israel. Blow the ram's horn and shout, 'Long live King Solomon!' Then escort him back here,

and he will sit on my throne. He will succeed me as king, for I have appointed him to be ruler over Israel and Judah." "Amen!" Benaiah son of Jehoiada replied. "May the Lord, the God of my lord the king, decree that it happen. And may the Lord be with Solomon as he has been with you, my lord the king, and may he make Solomon's reign even greater than yours!"

So Zadok the priest, Nathan the prophet, Benaiah son of Jehoiada, and the king's bodyguard took Solomon down to Gihon Spring, with Solomon riding on King David's own mule. There Zadok the priest took the flask of olive oil from the sacred tent and anointed Solomon with the oil. Then they sounded the ram's horn and all the people shouted, "Long live King Solomon!" And all the people followed Solomon into Jerusalem, playing flutes and shouting for joy. The celebration was so joyous and noisy that the earth shook with the sound. Adonijah and his guests heard the celebrating and shouting just as they were finishing their banquet. When Joab heard the sound of the ram's horn, he asked, "What's going on? Why is the city in such an uproar?" And while he was still speaking, Jonathan son of Abiathar the priest arrived. "Come in," Adonijah said to him, "for you are a good man. You must have good news." "Not at all!" Jonathan replied. "Our lord King David has just declared Solomon king! The king sent him down to Gihon Spring with Zadok the priest, Nathan the prophet, and Benaiah son of Jehoiada, protected by the king's bodyguard. They had him ride on the king's own mule, and Zadok and Nathan have anointed him at Gihon Spring as the new king. They have just returned, and the whole city is celebrating and rejoicing. That's what all the noise is about. What's more, Solomon is now sitting on the royal throne as king. And all the royal officials have gone to King David and congratulated him, saying, 'May your God make Solomon's fame even greater than your own, and may Solomon's reign be even greater than yours!' *Then the king bowed his head in worship as he lay in his bed, and he said, 'Praise the Lord, the God of Israel, who today has chosen a successor to sit on my throne while I am still alive to see it.'"*

Then all of Adonijah's guests jumped up in panic from the banquet table and quickly scattered. Adonijah was afraid of Solomon, so he rushed to the sacred tent and grabbed onto the horns of the altar. Word soon reached Solomon that Adonijah had seized the horns of the altar in fear, and that he was pleading, "Let King Solomon swear today that he will not kill me!"

> Solomon replied, "If he proves himself to be loyal, not a hair on his head will be touched. But if he makes trouble, he will die." So King Solomon summoned Adonijah, and they brought him down from the altar. He came and bowed respectfully before King Solomon, who dismissed him, saying, "Go on home" (1 Kings 1:28–53, NLT; emphasis added).

King David got up one last time to make certain that the throne would be passed on to his and Bathsheba's son, Solomon, as the Lord had spoken. Then he rejoiced in the Lord and finished his race strong! We will need to abide in Christ daily for spiritual nourishment in order to recover our strength, as we learned that King David repeatedly did.

> Give us this day our daily bread (Matthew 6:11, NIV).

> Then Jesus declared, "I am the bread of life. Whoever comes to me will never go hungry, and whoever believes in me will never be thirsty" (John 6:35, NIV).

> Yes, I am the vine; you are the branches. Those who remain in me, and I in them, will produce much fruit. For apart from me you can do

nothing" (John 15:5, NLT; emphasis added).

Will you learn from King David's life and unleash the power of momentum in your own life starting right now?

Chapter Fourteen

WHO WOULD EVER HAVE GUESSED?

During the reign of King Xerxes, the Jewish people were living in diaspora in Persia, an empire that stretched from India to Ethiopia, covering a large part of the known world at that time. After losing a war, many Jews had been taken as slaves to Babylon, which was subsequently overtaken by Persia. Two cousins named Mordecai and Esther would later become great leaders in this vast empire. They are about to give us some more valuable lessons on igniting momentum to defeat even the fiercest of foes. They had kept things moving forward in their lives after overcoming devastating losses in their family and nation. They both went on to achieve huge success.

> At that time there was a Jewish man in the fortress of Susa whose name was Mordecai son of Jair. He was from the tribe of Benjamin and was a descendant of Kish and Shimei. His family had been among those who, with King Jehoiachin of Judah, had been exiled from Jerusalem to

> Babylon by King Nebuchadnezzar. This man had a very beautiful and lovely young cousin, Hadassah, who was also called Esther. When her father and mother died, Mordecai adopted her into his family and raised her as his own daughter (Esther 2: 5–7, NLT).

The actions taken by Mordecai to protect his young cousin, Esther, after she lost both parents at such a young age, reveal to us the depth of his compassionate heart and virtuous character. He helped Esther to move on after a most difficult period in her young life by adopting her into his own family. So, our first takeaway from their story is,

We cannot undo the past, but we must endeavor to push past any devastating experiences that we might have had and move our lives forward.

Doing all that we can to not remain stuck in a state of depression or despair can only be accomplished through God's grace. We need His strength daily during both the good and the bad times, but most especially when we have suffered traumatic losses, as Esther did. Despite all our modern scientific advances, death cannot be reversed by human beings. So, I tenderly implore us to intentionally initiate actions that will help us to recover when we've had to deal with situations such as these. For I can do everything through Christ, who gives me strength (Philippians 4:13, NLT). We will be learning more about how this courageous young woman's actions and humble attitude eventually led her to unimaginable success in a country in which she had been originally taken captive as a slave. Another takeaway is this:

> *Make a habit of using your God-given blessings to help others as often as you possibly can.*

Mordecai did this, and we should too. Primarily because it is the loving and blessed way to live; not for any selfish motives of receiving anything back from those whom we bless. God promises to reward our acts of generosity towards Him and others. "Give, and you will receive. Your gift will return to you in full—pressed down, shaken together to make room for more, running over, and poured into your lap. The amount you give will determine the amount you get back" (Luke 6:38, NLT).

> Oh, the joys of those who are kind to the poor! The LORD rescues them when they are in trouble. The LORD protects them and keeps them alive. He gives them prosperity in the land and rescues them from their enemies. The LORD nurses them when they are sick and restores them to health (Psalm 41:1–3, NLT).

> Whoever is kind to the poor lends to the LORD, and he will reward them for what they have done (Proverbs 19:17, NIV).

> And I have been a constant example of how you can help those in need by working hard. You should remember the words of the Lord Jesus: *'It is more blessed to give than to receive'* (Acts 20:35, NLT; emphasis added).

As I already mentioned, we must not do our good deeds with any expectation of rewards from others, or to manipulate them. But it is wise to keep in mind that people whom we may have helped in the past, could end up wielding great power in the future. They might unexpectedly become instruments in God's hand to release His blessings into our lives. This proved to be the case for Mordecai. After adopting Esther into his family, a most unusual thing happened that catapulted his beautiful adopted daughter into the limelight and to heights of success, fame, and power that would have been unimaginable to either of them while she was growing up. King Xerxes suddenly had a major falling out with his Queen, named Vashti, and the breakup of their marriage resulted in her being deposed from her throne, and the process of Esther's amazing elevation started (see Esther 1).

But after Xerxes' anger had subsided, he began thinking about Vashti and what she had done and the decree he had made. So his personal attendants suggested, "Let us search the empire to find beautiful young virgins for the king. Let the king appoint agents in each province to bring these beautiful young women into the royal harem at the fortress of Susa. Hegai, the king's eunuch in charge of the harem, will see that they are all given beauty treatments. After that, the young woman who most pleases the king will be made queen instead of Vashti." This advice was very appealing to the king, so he put the plan into effect. As a result of the king's decree, Esther, along with many other young women, was brought to the king's harem at the fortress of Susa and placed in Hegai's care. Hegai was very impressed with Esther and treated her kindly. He quickly ordered a special menu for her and provided her with beauty treatments. He also assigned her seven maids specially chosen from the king's palace, and he moved her and her maids into the best place in the harem. Esther had not told anyone of her nationality and family background, because Mordecai had directed her not to do so.

Every day Mordecai would take a walk near the courtyard of the harem to find out about

Esther and what was happening to her. Before each young woman was taken to the king's bed, she was given the prescribed twelve months of beauty treatments—six months with oil of myrrh, followed by six months with special perfumes and ointments. When it was time for her to go to the king's palace, she was given her choice of whatever clothing or jewelry she wanted to take from the harem. That evening she was taken to the king's private rooms, and the next morning she was brought to the second harem, where the king's wives lived. There she would be under the care of Shaashgaz, the king's eunuch in charge of the concubines. She would never go to the king again unless he had especially enjoyed her and requested her by name.

Esther was the daughter of Abihail, who was Mordecai's uncle. (Mordecai had adopted his younger cousin Esther.) When it was Esther's turn to go to the king, she accepted the advice of Hegai, the eunuch in charge of the harem. She asked for nothing except what he suggested, and she was admired by everyone who saw her. Esther was taken to King Xerxes at the royal palace in early winter of the seventh year of his reign. And the king loved Esther more than any of the other young women. He was so delighted with her that he set the royal crown on her head and declared her queen instead of Vashti. To celebrate the occasion, he gave a great banquet in Esther's honor for all his nobles and officials, declaring a public holiday for the provinces and giving generous gifts to everyone. Even after all the young women had been transferred to the second harem and Mordecai had become a palace official, Esther continued to keep her family background and nationality a secret. She was still following Mordecai's directions, just as she did when she lived in his home, (Esther 2: 1–4, 8–20, NLT).

Of all the beautiful women in the land, Esther suddenly found herself crowned the new queen of Persia. Greatness had been thrust upon her, and this wise young woman rose to the challenge. Who could ever have guessed that while Mordecai was raising his young cousin, he was actually raising the next queen of Persia!

We must take the raising of our children most seriously. We never know what places of great honor that God might be taking them.

Mordecai could never have imagined that Esther would one day become the most powerful woman in the country to which they had been taken as slaves. As reiterated during our discussion, we must keep things moving forward just as Esther and Mordecai did after experiencing tragic losses. Doing this will help us to consistently experience success in our lives. These two cousins had learned to put the past behind them and make the best of the circumstances in which they had found themselves.

> But one thing I do: Forgetting what is behind and straining toward what is ahead (Philippians 3:13, NIV).

Queen Esther personifies a great saying by the English playwright William Shakespeare from his play *Twelfth Night*.

> *"Some are born great, some achieve greatness, and some have greatness thrust upon them."*

Both Mordecai and Queen Esther also exhibited another beautiful character trait, *humility*. Because Mordecai did not start throwing his weight around when his adopted daughter achieved the highest level of success in Persia. Esther also continued to respectfully follow her uncle's advice as she had done while living in his house, although she was now the queen of Persia—a position that must have been way beyond any of their wildest expectations or dreams. This is a virtue that we must all embrace. Esther was now the most powerful woman in the land, but she continued to willingly submit herself to the loving authority of her only surviving parental figure, Mordecai. These two are really admirable, don't you think? Esther's humble attitude would prove to be lifesaving for her and her people later on.

> Pride ends in humiliation, while humility brings honor (Proverbs 29:23, NLT).

> In the same way, you who are younger must accept the authority of the elders. And all of you, dress yourselves in humility as you relate to one another, for "God opposes the proud but gives grace to the humble." So humble yourselves under the mighty power of God, and at the right time he will lift you up in honor (1 Peter 5:5–6, NLT).

We're about to learn more about the depth of Mordecai's virtuous character and his loyalty toward the King of Persia from an incident that took place not long after Esther became the Queen. From that event, we will observe that although he was a slave of the Persian Empire and living in exile, Mordecai had no grudges against the authorities in Persia. This is important for us to know because a great misfortune would later befall the Jews through some actions taken by Mordecai.

> One day as Mordecai was on duty at the king's gate, two of the king's eunuchs, Bigthana and Teresh—who were guards at the door of the king's private quarters—became angry at King Xerxes and plotted to assassinate him. But Mordecai heard about the plot and gave the information to Queen Esther. She then told the king about it and gave Mordecai credit for the report. When an investigation was made and Mordecai's story was found to be true, the two men were impaled on a sharpened pole. This was all recorded in *The Book of the History of King Xerxes' Reign* (Esther 2: 21–23, NLT).

A loyal man of faith and courage, Mordecai proved through his actions that he didn't just talk the talk, but that he also walked the walk. And God was about to give him a taste of the many blessings that were in store for this humble man. He did this by keeping the King of Persia awake one night and guiding him to read the meritorious deed done by Mordecai for which he had not yet been rewarded.

> That night the king had trouble sleeping, so he ordered an attendant to bring the book of the history of his reign so it could be read to him. In those records he discovered an account of how Mordecai had exposed the plot of

Bigthana and Teresh, two of the eunuchs who guarded the door to the king's private quarters. They had plotted to assassinate King Xerxes. "What reward or recognition did we ever give Mordecai for this?" the king asked. His attendants replied, "Nothing has been done for him." "Who is that in the outer court?" the king inquired. As it happened, Haman had just arrived in the outer court of the palace to ask the king to impale Mordecai on the pole he had prepared. So the attendants replied to the king, "Haman is out in the court." "Bring him in," the king ordered. So Haman came in, and the king said, "What should I do to honor a man who truly pleases me?"

Haman thought to himself, "Whom would the king wish to honor more than me?" So he replied, "If the king wishes to honor someone, he should bring out one of the king's own royal robes, as well as a horse that the king himself has ridden—one with a royal emblem on its head. Let the robes and the horse be handed over to one of the king's most noble officials. And let him see that the man whom the king wishes to honor is dressed in the king's robes and led through the city square on the king's horse. Have the official shout as they go, 'This is what the king does for someone he wishes to honor!" "Excellent!" the king said to Haman. "Quick! Take the robes and my horse, and do just as you have said for Mordecai the Jew, who sits at the gate of the palace. Leave out nothing you have suggested!" So Haman took the robes and put them on Mordecai, placed him on the king's own horse, and led him through the city square, shouting, "This is what the king does for someone he wishes to honor!" Afterward Mordecai returned to the palace gate, but Haman hurried home dejected and completely humiliated (Esther 6: 1–12, NLT).

Check that out. What were the odds that among all the countless numbers of governmental records in their great library, it would be the one about Mordecai's unrewarded good deed that the King's attendant would randomly pull out of the stack! This could only be God's hand at work. He surely is a rewarder of those who diligently seek Him.

> And without faith it is impossible to please God, because anyone who comes to him must believe that he exists and that he rewards those who earnestly seek him (Hebrews 11:6, NIV).

> "Humble yourselves before the Lord, and he will lift you up in honor" (James 4:10, NLT).

Most especially when we least feel like doing so, we need to practice humility, generosity, and loyalty as Mordecai did. Do you agree?

Chapter Fifteen

FIRST CONNECT WITH GOD THROUGH PRAYERS

Quite unexpectedly and completely out of the blue, one day not too long after Esther had been crowned the new queen of Persia, a fierce attack came against the Jews from no less than the country's Prime Minister, Haman. He advised the king to sign an irrevocable decree that called for the immediate extermination of all the Jews living in Persia. Haman had decided to rise up against the Jews for the most outrageous of reasons—his pride and self-discontent. And once a Persian law had been sealed by the king of Persia, it was impossible to change it.

> For no document written in the king's name and sealed with his ring can be revoked (Esther 8:8, NIV).

The standoff between Haman and the Jews had begun when Queen Esther's cousin, Mordecai, offended Haman by refusing to participate in a widely accepted practice to honor the prime minister. Because Mordecai felt that the practice clashed with his faith and decided not to participate. He exercised his freedom to worship, not as a Persian official wanted him to, but as he believed that God wanted him to. Haman was so infuriated that he decided that Mordecai had shown him great disrespect and that he must punish him. But instead of punishing Mordecai alone, Haman decided to have all the Jews in Persia exterminated. Although Mordecai was a Jew, none of the other Jews had offended Prime Minister Haman, yet he sought the King's approval to kill them all. Here is how it happened:

> Sometime later King Xerxes promoted Haman son of Hammedatha the Agagite over all the other nobles, making him the most powerful official in the empire. All the king's officials would bow down before Haman to show him respect whenever he passed by, for so the king had commanded. But Mordecai refused to bow down or show him respect. Then the palace officials at the king's gate asked Mordecai, "Why are you disobeying the king's command?" They spoke to him day after day, but still he refused to comply with the order. So they spoke to Haman about this to see if he would tolerate Mordecai's conduct, as Mordecai had told them he was a Jew. When Haman saw that Mordecai would not bow down or show him respect, he was filled with rage.

He had learned of Mordecai's nationality, so he decided it was not enough to lay hands on Mordecai alone. Instead, he looked for a way to destroy all the Jews throughout the entire empire of Xerxes. So in the month of April, during the twelfth year of King Xerxes' reign, lots were cast in Haman's presence (the lots were called *purim*) to determine the best day and month to take action. And the day selected was March 7, nearly a year later. Then Haman approached King Xerxes and said, "There is a certain race of people scattered through all the provinces of your empire who keep themselves separate from everyone else. Their laws are different from those of any other people, and they refuse to obey the laws of the king. So it is not in the king's interest to let them live. If it please the king, issue a decree that they be destroyed, and I will give 10,000 large sacks of silver to the government administrators to be deposited in the royal treasury." The king agreed, confirming his decision by removing his signet ring from his finger and giving it to Haman son of Hammedatha the Agagite, the enemy of the Jews. The king said, "The money and the people are both yours to do with as you see fit." So on April 17 the king's secretaries were summoned, and a decree was written exactly as Haman dictated. It was sent to the king's highest officers, the governors of the respective provinces, and the nobles of each province in their own scripts and languages.

The decree was written in the name of King Xerxes and sealed with the king's signet ring. Dispatches were sent by swift messengers into all the provinces of the empire, giving the order that all Jews—young and old, including women and children—must be killed, slaughtered, and annihilated on a single day. This was scheduled to happen on March 7 of the next year. The property of the Jews would be given to those who killed them. A copy of this decree was to be issued as law in every province and proclaimed to all peoples, so that they would be ready to do their duty on the appointed day. At the king's command, the decree went out by swift messengers, and it was also proclaimed in the fortress of Susa. Then the king and Haman sat down to drink, but the city of Susa fell into confusion (Esther 3: 1–15, NLT).

After listening to the counsel of his top adviser, without knowing that his new queen was also a Jew, or investigating why his prime minister had made such a cruel demand, King Xerxes made a horrendous and irreversible error. The Jews found themselves *stuck* in a most frightening predicament. With her own and the death of all her people imminent, Queen Esther was facing an impossible situation. Haman's plot to exterminate all the Jews living in the Persian Empire would have annihilated virtually all the Jewish people in the known world at that time. Because the Persian Empire, which reached its greatest extent during Esther's time, had absorbed most of the lands of Assyria and Babylon, from where the Jews had originally been forcibly taken as slaves. So, how would the Jews get themselves unstuck from this impossible situation? How could the new Jewish queen use her position to help her people revoke an irrevocable law? They would need a miracle. All the Jews in the country were distraught. Both young and old, male and female, regardless of their social or economic status, were under this evil sentence. There are so many lessons to be drawn from this situation. But the most important is this:

When a situation looks impossible to us, it is not impossible for God!

For nothing will be impossible with God (Luke 1:37, ESV).

Is anything too hard for the LORD? (Genesis 18:14, NIV).

Jesus looked at them intently and said, "Humanly speaking, it is impossible. But not with God.

Everything is possible with God" (Mark 10:27, NLT).

Haman's evil and vicious plot to exterminate all the Jews in Persia was in direct opposition to the plan of God. His only begotten son, Jesus Christ, who would be the Savior of the whole world, was to come through the Jewish people and be a direct descendant of King David, as we learned earlier. So, King Xerxes' irrevocable law could not stand before God as it was written and sealed. The King of Kings—God almighty Himself—would have to overrule this earthly king, who was attempting to exterminate a people with a God-given promise.

The Persian King had ignorantly and inadvertently created a major stalemate between his empire and the creator of the universe!

You can make many plans, but the LORD's purpose will prevail (Proverbs 19:21, NLT).

The LORD frustrates the plans of the nations and thwarts all their schemes. The LORD's plans stand firm forever; his intentions can never be shaken (Psalm 33:10–11, NLT).

We can make our own plans, but the LORD gives the right answer (Proverbs 16:1, NLT).

*But how on earth does one revoke
an irrevocable law?*

Especially when God Himself had made it clear in His word that we must be law-abiding citizens, respecting the laws and authorities that govern the areas where we live.

> Everyone must submit to governing authorities. For all authority comes from God, and those in positions of authority have been placed there by God. So anyone who rebels against authority is rebelling against what God has instituted, and they will be punished (Romans 13:1–2, NLT).

> Remind the people to be subject to rulers and authorities, to be obedient, to be ready to do whatever is good (Titus 3:1, NIV).

Well, these two cousins are about to show us exactly how to do this. Mordecai and Queen Esther took up this monumental challenge and left us all with some priceless lessons on how to achieve success in spiritual and other kinds of warfare. The courage that these two displayed in the face of such a great calamity made them instrumental in the plan of God to save all the Jews and humanity as a whole, from all our sins.

> For we are not fighting against flesh-and-blood enemies, but against evil rulers and authorities of the unseen world, against mighty powers in this dark world, and against evil spirits in the heavenly places. Therefore, put on every piece of God's armor so you will be able to resist the enemy in the time of evil. Then after the battle you will still be standing firm (Ephesians 6:12–13, NLT).

Mordecai's seemingly disrespectful actions towards Haman had been based purely on his reverence for God. He believed that he could only bow in worship to God and not to any human being. So, God would have to be the one to whom both Queen Esther and Mordecai would run to for help.

> *The only force that is more powerful than human activity is God's power.*

These two cousins refused to stay stuck under King Xerxes' irrevocable law, and immediately ignited *momentum* by calling on all Jewish people living in the great Persian Empire to set apart a time for national prayers and fasting.

> "Go, gather together all the Jews who are in Susa, and fast for me. Do not eat or drink for

three days, night or day. I and my attendants will fast as you do. When this is done, I will go to the king, even though it is against the law. And if I perish, I perish." So Mordecai went away and carried out all Esther's instructions. (Esther 4:16–17, NIV.

Prayer unleashes momentum by connecting us to God and His limitless power.

Prayer gives us access to His grace and strength to help us to triumph over life's most difficult adversities and trials. As we've already learned, what looks impossible to us is not impossible for God.

We can say with confidence, "The LORD is my helper, so I will have no fear. What can mere people do to me? (Hebrews 13:6, NLT).

We're reminded once again from all these actions of Esther and Mordecai, that seeking God through our prayers is a powerful way to create momentum when we're at a dead end. Although they were facing what looked like a completely hopeless situation, Mordecai and Esther—and all the Jewish people living in Persia at that time—made the first decisive strike against this horrendous decree. They plugged their faith into God, appealing to Him for help. This act of faith is the right decision for anyone to make if they're suddenly faced with an unexpected challenge in their lives. The earthly reality at that time was that the King's decree could not be changed. But the people still chose to call upon God for His direct intervention. They had made their appeal to the highest sovereign of all, He who rules over all the affairs of human beings and His creation.

> But in my distress I cried out to the LORD; yes, I prayed to my God for help. He heard me from his sanctuary; my cry to him reached his ears (Psalm 18:6, NLT).

The Jews were not going to just give up and die because an earthly king said so. God almighty was their Ebenezer (which means "the stone of help"). He was about to come to His people's rescue by unleashing *divine momentum* against this irrevocable decree calling for their genocide.

> Samuel then took a large stone and placed it between the towns of Mizpah and Jeshanah. He named it Ebenezer (which means "the stone of help"), for he said, "Up to this point the LORD has helped us!" (1 Samuel 7:12, NLT).

> Then call on me when you are in trouble, and I will rescue you, and you will give me glory (Psalm 50:15, NLT).

Another takeaway from this? Whatever form that your own challenges may take, intentionally and immediately initiate the process of getting yourself unstuck by seeking God for His help.

> *Will you do this for yourself or others if it becomes necessary?*

Chapter Sixteen

THEN PARTY

We learned earlier that setting things into motion as fast as possible in positive ways can help us to get unstuck. This was exactly what these two, Mordecai and Esther, did. They created momentum by calling for national prayers and fasting among the Jews, and we'll soon be finding out what followed their prayers. God will never disappoint His believing children, and He did not disappoint these two and the Jewish people who had cried out to Him. After completing their prayers and fasting, on the third day Queen Esther followed through with corresponding *actions*.

> On the third day of the fast, Esther put on her royal robes and entered the inner court of the palace, just across from the king's hall. The king was sitting on his royal throne, facing the entrance. When he saw Queen Esther standing there in the inner court, he welcomed her and held out the gold scepter to her. So Esther approached and touched the end of the scepter. Then the king asked her, "What do you want, Queen Esther? What is your request? I will

give it to you, even if it is half the kingdom!" And Esther replied, "If it please the king, let the king and Haman come today to a banquet I have prepared for the king." The king turned to his attendants and said, "Tell Haman to come quickly to a banquet, as Esther has requested." So the king and Haman went to Esther's banquet. And while they were drinking wine, the king said to Esther, "Now tell me what you really want. What is your request? I will give it to you, even if it is half the kingdom!"

Esther replied, "This is my request and deepest wish. If I have found favor with the king, and if it pleases the king to grant my request and do what I ask, please come with Haman tomorrow to the banquet I will prepare for you. Then I will explain what this is all about." Haman was a happy man as he left the banquet! But when he saw Mordecai sitting at the palace gate, not standing up or trembling nervously before him, Haman became furious. However, he restrained himself and went on home. Then Haman gathered together his friends and Zeresh, his wife, and boasted to them about his great wealth and his many children. He bragged about the honors the king had given him and how he had been promoted over all the other nobles and officials. Then Haman added, "And that's not all! Queen Esther invited only me and the king himself to the banquet she prepared for us. And she has invited me to dine with her and the king again tomorrow!" Then he added, "But this is all worth nothing as long as I see Mordecai the Jew just sitting there at the palace gate."

So Haman's wife, Zeresh, and all his friends suggested, "Set up a sharpened pole that stands seventy-five feet tall, and in the morning ask the king to impale Mordecai on it. When this is done, you can go on your merry way to the banquet with the king." This pleased Haman, and he ordered the pole set up (Esther 5: 1–14, NLT).

So the king and Haman went to Queen Esther's banquet. On this second occasion, while they were drinking wine, the king again said to Esther, "Tell me what you want, Queen Esther. What is your request? I will give it to you, even if it is half the kingdom!" Queen Esther replied, "If I have found favor with the king, and if it pleases the king to grant my request, I ask that my life and the lives of my people will be spared. For my people and I have been sold to those who would kill, slaughter, and annihilate us. If we had merely been sold as slaves, I could remain quiet, for that would be too trivial a matter to warrant disturbing the king." "Who would do such a thing?" King Xerxes demanded. "Who would be so presumptuous as to touch you?" Esther replied, "This wicked Haman is our adversary and our enemy." Haman grew pale with fright before the king and queen. Then the king jumped to his feet in a rage and went out into the palace garden. Haman, however, stayed behind to plead for his life with Queen Esther, for he knew that the king intended to kill him.

In despair he fell on the couch where Queen Esther was reclining, just as the king was returning from the palace garden. The king exclaimed, "Will he even assault the queen right here in the palace, before my very eyes?" And as soon as the king spoke, his attendants covered Haman's face, signaling his doom. Then Harbona, one of the king's eunuchs, said, "Haman has set up a sharpened pole that stands seventy-five feet tall in his own courtyard. He intended to use it to impale Mordecai, the man who saved the king from assassination." "Then impale Haman on it!" the king ordered. So they impaled Haman on the pole he had set up for Mordecai, and the king's anger subsided (Esther 7: 1–10, NLT).

Wow, what an amazing turnaround of events! After seeking His help, God gave Queen Esther wisdom and a divine strategy on how to approach her powerful husband, King Xerxes. One would never have guessed that inviting him to a private party with her enemy would be the method through which this brave young woman would overcome this unquantifiable disaster for her and her people. God had granted Esther favor with the king and gave her resounding victory over the evil plot with a counter decree. Hallelujah! So, here is our next lesson:

*God will always have the final say in
all circumstances and situations.*

He got the Jews unstuck because they believed in Him, and refused to stay stuck under an irrevocable decree. They sought God for His help, igniting momentum through their prayers and fasting. The Jewish people were able to reverse the genocidal plan of their enemy with God's help and the rest, as they say, is history! There are always spoils of war after winning a battle, and this conflict was no exception. Mordecai got a big fat promotion and, check this out:

> On that same day King Xerxes gave the property of Haman, the enemy of the Jews, to Queen Esther. Then Mordecai was brought before the king, for Esther had told the king how they were related. The king took off his signet ring—which he had taken back from Haman—and gave it to Mordecai. And Esther appointed Mordecai to

be in charge of Haman's property. Then Esther went again before the king, falling down at his feet and begging him with tears to stop the evil plot devised by Haman the Agagite against the Jews. Again the king held out the gold scepter to Esther. So she rose and stood before him. Esther said, "If it please the king, and if I have found favor with him, and if he thinks it is right, and if I am pleasing to him, let there be a decree that reverses the orders of Haman son of Hammedatha the Agagite, who ordered that Jews throughout all the king's provinces should be destroyed. For how can I endure to see my people and my family slaughtered and destroyed?" Then King Xerxes said to Queen Esther and Mordecai the Jew, "I have given Esther the property of Haman, and he has been impaled on a pole because he tried to destroy the Jews. Now go ahead and send a message to the Jews in the king's name, telling them whatever you want, and seal it with the king's signet ring. But remember that whatever has already been written in the king's name and sealed with his signet ring can never be revoked." So on June 25 the king's secretaries were summoned, and a decree was written exactly as Mordecai dictated. It was sent to the Jews and to the highest officers, the governors, and the nobles of all the 127 provinces stretching from India to Ethiopia. The decree was written in the scripts and languages of all the peoples of the empire, including that of the Jews. The decree was written in the name of King Xerxes and sealed with the king's signet ring. Mordecai sent the dispatches by swift messengers, who rode fast horses especially bred for the king's service.

The king's decree gave the Jews in every city authority to unite to defend their lives. They were allowed to kill, slaughter, and annihilate anyone of any nationality or province who might attack them or their children and wives, and to take the property of their enemies. The day chosen for this event throughout all the provinces of King Xerxes was March 7 of the next year. A copy of this decree was to be issued as law in every province and proclaimed to all peoples, so that the Jews would be ready to take revenge on their enemies on the appointed day. So urged on by the king's command, the messengers rode out swiftly on fast horses bred for the king's service. The same decree was also proclaimed in the fortress of Susa. Then Mordecai left the king's presence, wearing the royal robe of blue and white, the great crown of gold, and an outer cloak of fine linen and purple. And the people of Susa celebrated the new decree.

The Jews were filled with joy and gladness and were honored everywhere. In every province and city, wherever the king's decree arrived, the Jews rejoiced and had a great celebration and declared a public festival and holiday. And many of the people of the land became Jews themselves, for they feared what the Jews might do to them (Esther 8:1–15, NLT).

So the Jews went ahead on the appointed day and struck down their enemies with the sword. They killed and annihilated their enemies and did as they pleased with those who hated them. In the fortress of Susa itself, the Jews killed 500 men. They also killed Parshandatha, Dalphon, Aspatha, Poratha, Adalia, Aridatha, Parmashta, Arisai, Aridai, and Vaizatha—the ten sons of Haman son of Hammedatha, the enemy of the Jews. But they did not take any plunder. That very day, when the king was informed of the number of people killed in the fortress of Susa, he called for Queen Esther. He said, "The Jews have killed 500 men in the fortress of Susa alone, as well as Haman's ten sons. If they have done that here, what has happened in the rest of the provinces? But now, what more do you want? It will be granted to you; tell me and I will do it." Esther responded, "If it please the king, give the

Jews in Susa permission to do again tomorrow as they have done today, and let the bodies of Haman's ten sons be impaled on a pole." So the king agreed, and the decree was announced in Susa. And they impaled the bodies of Haman's ten sons. Then the Jews at Susa gathered together on March 8 and killed 300 more men, and again they took no plunder (Esther 9:5–15, NLT).

"And this same God who takes care of me will supply all your needs from his glorious riches, which have been given to us in Christ Jesus" (Philippians 4:19, NLT). Amen. Nothing is ever too difficult for God. So, don't delay inviting our loving creator to intervene on your own behalf in your challenging situation. God's character is love. His willingness to help His children is undoubtable. If necessary, add fasting from food or a favorite daily routine or activity for a specific amount of time to your prayers, as you're medically approved and physically able to do.

Will you begin today to seek God for His help through your prayers?

Chapter Seventeen

Feeling like the Olives in the Press?

In the Bible, oil is a widely understood symbol of the Holy Spirit. The Spirit of the Lord and the oil of anointing are directly linked.

> Then the LORD said to Moses, "Collect choice spices—12½ pounds of pure myrrh, 6¼ pounds of fragrant cinnamon, 6¼ pounds of fragrant calamus, and 12½ pounds of cassia—as measured by the weight of the sanctuary shekel. Also get one gallon of olive oil. Like a skilled incense maker, blend these ingredients to make a holy anointing oil. Use this sacred oil to anoint the Tabernacle, the Ark of the Covenant, the table and all its utensils, the lampstand and all its accessories, the incense altar, the altar of burnt offering and all its utensils, and the washbasin with its stand. Consecrate them to make them absolutely holy. After this, whatever touches them will also become holy. "Aaron and his sons also, consecrating them to serve me as priests. And say to

the people of Israel, 'This holy anointing oil is reserved for me from generation to generation. It must never be used to anoint anyone else, and you must never make any blend like it for yourselves. It is holy, and you must treat it as holy. Anyone who makes a blend like it or anoints someone other than a priest will be cut off from the community'" (Exodus 30:22–33, NLT).

The Spirit of the Lord is upon me, for he has anointed me to bring Good News to the poor. He has sent me to proclaim that captives will be released, that the blind will see, that the oppressed will be set free (Luke 4:18, NLT).

Oftentimes, the only way that human beings will discover the depth of the courage, gifts, and attributes that God has placed within them is when they're facing the most severe pressures.

Just try to picture the amount of pressure that the large granite stones that were traditionally used in the early days to crush olives must have had. Modern olive mills are partially or fully automated, so the granite crushers have been replaced with stainless steel ones that can rotate at very high speed. Whether it's the traditional or modern method that is used, olives must be crushed in order to extract their oil. And I don't think that anyone volunteers for this crushing process. But the most beautiful oil (anointing) that can be released through our lives may have to come through an experience that might make us feel as if we're being completely crushed.

The ultimate example of this level of brokenness can be closely observed through what our Lord and Savior, Jesus Christ, had to endure in order to pay for all human beings' sins. He went through the most excruciating death on a cross to redeem us all.

> Yet it was our weaknesses He carried;
> > it was our sorrows that weighed Him down.
> And we thought his troubles were a punishment from God,
> > a punishment for His own sins!
> But He was pierced for our rebellion,
> > *crushed for our sins.*
> He was beaten so we could be whole.
> He was whipped so we could be healed.
> All of us, like sheep, have strayed away.
> We have left God's paths to follow our own.
> Yet the Lord laid on Him the sins of us all.
> He was oppressed and treated harshly,
> > yet He never said a word.
> He was led like a lamb to the slaughter.
> And as a sheep is silent before the shearers,
> He did not open his mouth. Unjustly condemned,

He was led away.
No one cared that He died without descendants,
    that His life was cut short in midstream.
But He was struck down
    for the rebellion of my people.
He had done no wrong
    and had never deceived anyone.
But He was buried like a criminal;
He was put in a rich man's grave.
But it was the Lord's good plan to *crush Him*
    and cause Him grief.
Yet when His life is made an offering for sin,
He will have many descendants.
He will enjoy a long life,
    and the Lord's good plan will prosper in His hands.
When He sees all that is accomplished by His anguish,
He will be satisfied.
And because of His experience,
    my righteous servant will make it possible
    for many to be counted righteous,
    for He will bear all their sins
(Isaiah 53:4–11, NLT; emphasis added).

Accepting God's free offer of forgiveness makes us a part of His loving and divine family. Knowing this ought to remove any doubts

> *from our hearts about His love for us or His willingness to rescue us when we need Him.*

When God sent His only begotten son, Jesus Christ, into the world to pay for all of human beings' sins by dying on a cross, the *crushing blows* that He went through for our sakes brought all of us the free gift of salvation. Anyone who chooses to place their trust in Christ's sacrifice for their past, present, and future sins receives God's free pardon and eternal life.

> For God so [greatly] loved *and* dearly prized the world, that He [even] gave His [One and] only begotten Son, so that whoever believes *and* trusts in Him [as Savior] shall not perish, but have eternal life (John 3:16, AMP; brackets in the original).

> Jesus told her, "I am the resurrection and the life. Anyone who believes in me will live, even after dying" (John 11:25, NLT).

Don't hesitate to place your trust in God at all times, especially if you encounter any of life's most difficult adversities and trials. Trust that in His loving hands, our lives can produce far better results than we could ever do on our own. Wonderful blessings can still flow through us if we choose to respond correctly during any painful processes that we might have to endure. After our brokenness is over, we will be healed, restored, and transformed into vessels of great worth by God, so that we can bless many more lives than we could ever have imagined or desired to do.

> The Lord gave another message to Jeremiah. He said, "Go down to the potter's shop, and I will speak to you there." So, I did as he told me and found the potter working at his wheel. But the jar he was making did not turn out as he had hoped, so he *crushed* it into a lump of clay again and started over. Then the Lord gave me this message: "O Israel, can I not do to you as this potter has done to his clay? As the clay is in the potter's hand, so are you in my hand" (Jeremiah 18:1–6, NLT)

> Blessed [gratefully praised and adored] be the God and Father of our Lord Jesus Christ, the Father of mercies and the God of all comfort, who comforts and encourages us in every trouble so that we will be able to comfort and encourage those who are in any kind of trouble, with the comfort with which we ourselves are comforted by God (2 Corinthians 1:3–4, AMP; brackets in the original).

Due to the fallen state of our world, human beings may sometimes have to go through what might feel like crushing experiences in their lives. But these unwelcome experiences can be used by God to make our lives beautiful and completely new in ways beyond our capacity to comprehend, if we entrust ourselves to Him. And after all that Christ went through for our sakes, the scriptures inform us that God the Father rewarded Him in these ways:

> At the name of Jesus every knee should bow, in heaven and on earth and under the earth, and every tongue declare that Jesus Christ is Lord, to the glory of God the Father" (Philippians 2:10–11, NLT).

And God also said the following about Him:

> I will give him the honors of a victorious soldier, because he exposed himself to death. He was counted among the rebels. He bore the sins of many and interceded for rebels (Isaiah 53:12, NLT).

> I implore us to remain steadfast in our faith, especially when we do not understand all that God is doing or where He is taking us.

All that we go through is never wasted. Instead, it produces overflowing blessings into our own lives with which we can be generous to others.

And God will generously provide all you need. Then you will always have everything you need and plenty left over to share with others (2 Corinthians 9:8, NLT).

You prepare a feast for me in the presence of my enemies. You honor me by anointing my head with oil. My cup overflows with blessings (Psalm 23:5, NLT).

Therefore, since we have been made right in God's sight by faith, we have peace with God because of what Jesus Christ our Lord has done for us. Because of our faith, Christ has brought us into this place of undeserved privilege where we now stand, and we confidently and joyfully look forward to sharing God's glory. We can rejoice, too, when we run into problems and trials, for we know that they help us develop endurance. And endurance develops strength of character, and character strengthens our confident hope of salvation. And this hope will not lead to disappointment. For we know how dearly God loves us, because he has given us the Holy Spirit to fill our hearts with his love. When we were utterly helpless, Christ came at just the right time and died for us sinners (Romans 5:1–6, NLT).

Be assured that He will never allow us to go through anything for which His grace will not be more than sufficient for us. God has promised to bring us safely through life's darkest valleys and release overflowing blessings into our lives. "So, let's not get tired of doing what is good. At just the right time we will reap a harvest of blessing if we don't give up" (Galatians 6:9, NLT).

As beneficiaries of the great crushing that Jesus Christ went through for all human beings' sins, do you think that His great sacrifice was worth it?

Chapter Eighteen

Ask, Seek, and Knock

I believe that life is the most precious gift that we've been given by God. We're here on the planet to live as fully and with as much joy as possible! Although we may not always be able to fully understand God's ways, we must not doubt the depths of His incomprehensible love for all human beings. If we truly desire to experience nonstop progress in our lives, mending our broken relationship with God is the place to start. Seeking Him daily through His word and our prayers is irreplaceable in order to securely and successfully build our lives. Consequently, faith comes from hearing the message, and the message is heard through the word about Christ (Romans 10:17, NIV).

And it is impossible to please God without faith. Anyone who wants to come to him must believe that God exists and that he rewards those who sincerely seek him (Hebrews 11:6, NLT).

When we spend quality time with God, He promises to provide us with all that we need to grow stronger and triumph over all of life's circumstances and situations. God's Holy Spirit living on the inside of all His believing children helps us to grow in Godly wisdom and leads and guides us at all times.

> For all who are led by the Spirit of God are children of God. So you have not received a spirit that makes you fearful slaves. Instead, you received God's Spirit when he adopted you as his own children. Now we call him, "Abba, Father" (Romans 8:14–15, NLT).

> *Our loving creator does not force His will on anyone. He has given us the freedom to choose to love Him or not.*

Because it is not love if it is forced upon us. But God has granted all those who will accept His free offer of forgiveness a complete release from all guilt and condemnation. Start to reignite your momentum today by reconnecting with Him, and discover who you are and what you have been created for. If God sent His only begotten son into this world to save us, what could be more precious than this that He would withhold from us? "He who did not spare his own Son, but gave him up for us all—how will he not also, along with him, graciously give us all things?" (Romans 8:32, NIV).

So, fully realign yourself with God through His word in order to start to enjoy the abundant blessings that Jesus Christ died and paid for all human beings to receive. If you're accustomed to denying God's existence, defying Him, or making other poor spiritual choices, this will keep you stuck in your sins, and in negative habits and places. Repent of all these and mend your relationship with God. Then move forward with your new life in Christ.

> Repent, then, and turn to God, so that your sins may be wiped out, that times of refreshing may come from the Lord (Acts 3:19, NIV).

> When you pass through the waters, I will be with you; and through the rivers, they shall not overwhelm you; when you walk through fire you shall not be burned, and the flame shall not consume you. For I am the LORD your God, the Holy One of Israel, your Savior (Isaiah 43:2–3, ESV).

And if you have already been in a relationship with God for many years, ask God again for His help with whatever you're grappling with. Even if you have done so on many previous occasions.

*Seek God afresh and let your
trust in Him remain firm.*

We're encouraged to do this by Jesus in the following example. God is always ready and willing to help us. Simply seize the momentum and seek Him to receive all the abundant blessings that He has already prepared for you beforehand.

> Then Jesus said to them, "Suppose you have a friend, and you go to him at midnight and say, 'Friend, lend me three loaves of bread; a friend of mine on a journey has come to me, and I have no food to offer him.' And suppose the one inside answers, 'Don't bother me. The door is already locked, and my children and I are in bed. I can't get up and give you anything.' I tell you, even though he will not get up and give you the bread because of friendship, yet because of your shameless audacity he will surely get up and give you as much as you need. So, I say to you: Ask and it will be given to you; seek and you will find; knock and the door will be opened to you. *For everyone who asks receives; the one who seeks finds; and to the one who knocks, the door will be opened.*
>
> "Which of you fathers, if your son asks for a fish, will give him a snake instead? Or if he asks

for an egg, will give him a scorpion? If you then, though you are evil, know how to give good gifts to your children, how much more will your Father in heaven give the Holy Spirit to those who ask him!" (Luke 11:5–13, NIV; emphasis added).

Elijah, for another example, had to repeat the exercise of seeking God for an answer seven times. But he continued to seek God without wavering, because he believed that God would answer his prayers.

> Then Elijah said to Ahab, "Go get something to eat and drink, for I hear a mighty rainstorm coming!" So Ahab went to eat and drink. But Elijah climbed to the top of Mount Carmel and bowed low to the ground and prayed with his face between his knees. Then he said to his servant, "Go and look out toward the sea." The servant went and looked, then returned to Elijah and said, "I didn't see anything." *Seven times* Elijah told him to go and look. *Finally the seventh time,* his servant told him, "I saw a little cloud about the size of a man's hand rising from the sea." Then Elijah shouted, "Hurry to Ahab and tell him, 'Climb into your chariot and go back home. If you don't hurry, the rain will stop you!'" And soon the sky was black with clouds.

A heavy wind brought a terrific rainstorm, and Ahab left quickly for Jezreel. Then the Lord gave special strength to Elijah. He tucked his cloak into his belt and ran ahead of Ahab's chariot all the way to the entrance of Jezreel (1 Kings 18:41–46, NLT; emphasis added).

> *We're unable to know or see all the things that God is doing behind the scenes on our behalves. So, we must trust in Him.*

The four lepers that we read about earlier, and their entire country, certainly could not see what God was going to do on their behalves beforehand. They did not know that their desperate needs had already been met by Him. Their prayers had been answered, but no one knew anything about it yet. Had they not decided to set things in motion, their entire country would have continued to suffer and not known about God's miraculous provisions. It took four desperate lepers who must have felt completely crushed to finally make the amazing discovery. God is also working on your behalf. Don't allow the unpleasant interruptions to your own life to separate you further from Him. Because even when we cannot see His miraculous hands are at work behind the scenes. Even if we do not believe in Him, God still lovingly works on all human beings' behalves.

Jesus replied, My Father is always working, and so am I" (John 5:17, NLT).

Faith shows the reality of what we hope for; it is the evidence of things we cannot see (Hebrews 11:1, NLT).

I call upon the LORD, who is worthy to be praised, and I am saved from my enemies (Psalm 18:3, ESV).

If we will have faith in Him, take courage, and set things into motion as fast as possible, God will meet us at the point of our need in ways beyond our ability to dream or imagine. If the pressures that you're currently facing fall within the realms of temptation, God promises not to allow you to be tempted beyond your endurance.

> No temptation [regardless of its source] has overtaken or enticed you that is not common to human experience [nor is any temptation unusual or beyond human resistance]; but God is faithful [to His word—He is compassionate and trustworthy], and He will not let you be tempted beyond your ability [to resist], but along with the temptation He [has in the past and is now and] will [always] provide the way out as well, so that you will be able to endure it

> [without yielding, and will overcome temptation with joy] (1 Corinthians 10:13, AMP; brackets in the original).

"In my distress I cried out to the LORD; yes, I prayed to my God for help. He heard me from his sanctuary; my cry to him reached his ears" (Psalm 18:6, NLT). Just as Mordecai, Esther, and the Jews in Persia did, don't quit believing in God. Simply keep on asking, seeking, and knocking until you see observable changes in the issue at hand.

> Then Jesus told his disciples a parable to show them that *they should always pray and not give up.* He said: "In a certain town there was a judge who neither feared God nor cared what people thought. And there was a widow in that town who kept coming to him with the plea, 'Grant me justice against my adversary.'" For some time he refused. But finally he said to himself, 'Even though I don't fear God or care what people think, yet because this widow keeps bothering me, I will see that she gets justice, so that she won't eventually come and attack me!'" And the Lord said, "Listen to what the unjust judge says. *And will not God bring about justice for his chosen ones, who cry out to him day and night? Will he keep putting them off?* I tell you; he will see that they

get justice, and quickly. However, when the Son of Man comes, will he find faith on the earth?" (Luke 18:1–8, NIV; emphasis added).

I remind us that we have no idea what gems we might discover if we ignite momentum in our own situations instead of staying stuck.

> Are any of you suffering hardships? You should pray. Are any of you happy? You should sing praises (James 5:13, NLT).

> Then call on me when you are in trouble, and I will rescue you, and you will give me glory (Psalm 50:15, NLT).

We must keep on "fixing our eyes on Jesus, the pioneer and perfecter of faith. For the joy set before him he endured the cross, scorning its shame, and sat down at the right hand of the throne of God. Consider him who endured such opposition from sinners, so that you will not grow weary and lose heart" (Hebrews 12:2–3, NIV).

> *Will you fix your eyes on Jesus, the pioneer and perfecter of your faith and, at just the right time, receive a mighty harvest of blessings from God if you don't give up?*

Chapter Nineteen

Move On

Human beings usually want to see what God has promised before being willing to believe in Him. But God wants us to believe in Him first, then we will see what He has promised. "Therefore I say to you, whatever things you ask when you pray, believe that you receive them, and you will have them" (Mark 11:24, New King James Version). Sometimes, the pressures that we face make it difficult for us to believe that God is working on our behalves behind the scenes, when in fact, He might be blessing us with far greater miracles than the ones that we're asking Him for. A great example of severe pressure moving people in an unusual direction can be seen in another episode in the nation of Israel.

After being slaves in Egypt for over four hundred years, God had performed many miracles to help the Israelites escape from captivity. But not too long after their great escape, they suddenly found themselves caught between their old foe, Pharaoh, and his formidable army, and the great Red Sea. With no way of escape behind or ahead of them, the massive crowd found themselves stuck with only two options: either to die at the hand of their fierce and enraged enemies—Pharaoh and his mighty military forces—or drown in the great Red Sea. The calamitous situation placed unbearable pressure on the people, and they all cried out to their leader Moses.

> When the king of Egypt was told that the people had fled, Pharaoh and his officials changed their minds about them and said, "What have we done? We have let the Israelites go and have lost their services!" So, he had his chariot made ready and took his army with him. He took six hundred of the best chariots, along with all the other chariots of Egypt, with officers over all of them. The Lord hardened the heart of Pharaoh King of Egypt, so that he pursued the Israelites, who were marching out boldly. The Egyptians—all Pharaoh's horses and chariots, horsemen and troops—pursued the Israelites and overtook them as they camped by the sea near Pi Hahiroth, opposite Baal Zephon. As Pharaoh approached, the Israelites looked up, and there were the Egyptians, marching after them. They were terrified and cried out to the Lord. They said to Moses, "Was it because there were no graves in Egypt that you brought us to the desert to die? What have you done to us by bringing us out of Egypt? Didn't we say to you in Egypt, 'Leave us alone; let us serve the Egyptians'? It would have been better for us to

serve the Egyptians than to die in the desert!" Moses answered the people, "Do not be afraid. Stand firm and you will see the deliverance the Lord will bring you today. The Egyptians you see today you will never see again. The Lord will fight for you; you need only to be still." Then the Lord said to Moses, "Why are you crying out to me?

Tell the Israelites to move on.

Raise your staff and stretch out your hand over the sea to divide the water so that the Israelites can go through the sea on dry ground. I will harden the hearts of the Egyptians so that they will go in after them. And I will gain glory through Pharaoh and all his army, through his chariots and his horsemen. The Egyptians will know that I am the Lord when I gain glory through Pharaoh, his chariots, and his horsemen." Then the angel of God, who had been traveling in front of Israel's army, withdrew and went behind them. The pillar of cloud also moved from in front and stood behind them, coming between the armies of Egypt and Israel. Throughout the night the cloud brought darkness to the one side and light to the other side; so neither went near the other all night long. Then Moses stretched out his hand over the sea, and all that night the Lord drove the sea back with a strong east wind and turned it into dry land. The waters were divided, and the Israelites went through the sea on dry ground, with a wall of water on their right and on their left. The Egyptians pursued them, and all Pharaoh's horses and chariots and horsemen followed them into the sea. During the last watch of the night the Lord looked down from the pillar of fire and cloud at the Egyptian army and threw it into confusion. He jammed the wheels of their chariots so that they had difficulty driving. And the Egyptians said, "Let's get away from the Israelites! The Lord is fighting for them against Egypt." Then the Lord said to Moses, "Stretch out your hand over the sea so that the waters may flow back over the Egyptians and their chariots and horsemen." Moses stretched out his hand over the sea, and at daybreak the sea went back to its place. The Egyptians were fleeing toward it, and the Lord swept them into the sea. The water flowed back and covered the chariots and horsemen—the entire army of Pharaoh that had followed the Israelites into the sea. Not one of them survived. But the Israelites went through the sea on dry ground, with a wall of water on their right and on their left (Exodus 14:5–29, NIV; emphasis added)

Moses had faith in God and acted upon the instruction that God had given to him. The people *moved forward* toward the Red Sea and thereby created momentum without knowing that they were activating a powerful principle of faith. First believe in what God has said in His word, then set things into motion by acting on it. No one had any idea exactly what would happen after they stepped into the red sea. But the severe pressure and no other visible options, forced the people to trust in God. They simply moved forward as God had told Moses. The four lepers had done the same thing in our earlier example, forcefully advancing although the road ahead appeared to hold no good options.

> Jesus responded, "Didn't I tell you that you would see God's glory if you believe?" (John 11:40, NLT).

Some of the people might have thought that God was about to drown them in the Red Sea because He couldn't deliver them as He had promised. But God again showed up big! The Israelites were not required to do anything other than to have faith in Him and *move forward*. God was the one who was going to part the Red Sea, and in God's way of doing things, He wants us to believe in Him and proceed, before we can see the wonderful blessings that He has prepared.

> *If we will start to consistently activate the powerful principle of momentum whenever we're feeling stuck, then doing nothing will no longer be an option for us.*

I sought the LORD [on the authority of His word], and He answered me, and delivered me from all my fears (Psalm 34:4, AMP; brackets in the original).

Take delight in the LORD, and he will give you your heart's desires (Psalm 37:4, NLT).

I will answer them before they even call to me. While they are still talking about their needs, I will go ahead and answer their prayers! (Isaiah 65:24, NLT).

I remind us again to start to set things into motion by fully trusting in God, as we just read that the Israelites did. He has promised to work all things together for our good. Through our faith in him and obedience to His instructions, we will find out that, "God is our refuge and strength, always ready to help in times of trouble" (Psalm 46:1, NLT), just as He did in the lives of the four poor lepers and these terrified Israelites when they all thought that their lives were over.

Therefore let all the faithful pray to you while you may be found; surely the rising of the mighty waters will not reach them (Psalm 32:6, NIV). Amen.

The severe pressure that they were under also revealed to all these people that there was great faith and courage lying deep within them that they might never have discovered that they possessed.

But against all odds, by simply moving forward based solely on their faith in God's word, and not knowing exactly what would happen, all these people received a mighty revelation of who God is. They had awesome encounters with His power, and the Israelites were once again rescued from their foes. "What other nation is so great as to have their gods near them the way the LORD our God is near us whenever we pray to him?" (Deuteronomy 4:7, NIV). They must have thought. God is also at work within each one of us and in our various circumstances. We do not have to rely solely on our own strength to pull through. If we're willing to place our trust in our invincible creator, we will be amazed by all that does on our behalves.

I pray that God, the source of hope, will fill you completely with joy and peace because you trust in him. Then you will overflow with confident hope through the power of the Holy Spirit (Romans 15:13, NLT). Amen.

And this hope will not lead to disappointment. For we know how dearly God loves us, because he has given us the Holy Spirit to fill our hearts with his love (Romans 5:5, NLT).

Despite the limited strength that we all possess as human beings, we can draw fresh strength from God daily, and get up and get going again. From the vantage point of eternity, I am certain that we will look back on all that we had to go through and have much cause to give God glory. I hope that the following words written by the prophet Jeremiah, after witnessing the destruction of his home and the forced exile of his people to Babylon, will help us to remember that even in the midst of great destruction, there is still a reason to have hope: God. Let us trust in Him. He will never fail or abandon us.

> The thought of my suffering and homelessness
>   is bitter beyond words.
> I will never forget this awful time,
>   as I grieve over my loss.
> Yet I still dare to hope
>   when I remember this:
> The faithful love of the Lord never ends!

> His mercies never cease.
> Great is his faithfulness;
> > his mercies begin afresh each morning.
> I say to myself, "The Lord is my inheritance;
> > therefore, I will hope in him!"
> The Lord is good to those who depend on him,
> > to those who search for him.
> So it is good to wait quietly
> > for salvation from the Lord.
> (Lamentations 3:19–26, NLT).

Begin today to take the necessary steps to get your own life back on track. Triumphing over what may look to us like unsurmountable odds begins with first getting unstuck in our own minds. Our nonstop progress is inextricably linked to creating and keeping up our momentum at all times and in all kinds of circumstances. "Jesus looked at them intently and said, 'Humanly speaking, it is impossible. But with God everything is possible'" (Matthew 19:26, NLT). So, let's get moving!

Are you willing to start taking the necessary steps toward getting yourself unstuck?

Chapter Twenty

REFUSE TO STAY STUCK

A poor widow in our next example again reminds us that creating momentum can be the start of great blessings in our lives. She refused to stay stuck in a dead-end situation when things looked completely bleak for her and her two sons. In her desperation, she decided to move things forward by seeking help from one of God's servants, a renowned prophet by the name of Elisha. There were limited ways for women to generate an income in those days, and most women's finances during their times were inextricably joined to those of their spouses. After her husband, who was a prophet by calling, passed away, his poor widow was left with no means of support for their family. He had left them in debt with no property, money, or any other useful assets to offset all their obligations. Their two sons were facing indentured servitude, which was a legal form of debt repayment in those days. This goes to show that with poor financial management, debt can accumulate in anyone's life, including God's servants—ministers.

We must all be careful to educate ourselves on good financial practices and apply them.

This lady, however, refused to just curl up and give up. Instead, she decided to ignite momentum by seeking God's help through His servant Elisha. This was the way that people sought God during her times. In our time, we can directly approach God for help, because of what His son Jesus Christ has done for us. "Because of Christ and our faith in him, we can now come boldly and confidently into God's presence" (Ephesians 3:12, NLT).

Decide today to put your trust in God, and use whatever tools that you have left at your disposal to advance. Then follow your decisions through with the necessary actions as we will be learning from this poor widow.

> One day the widow of a member of the group of prophets *came to* Elisha and cried out, "My husband who served you is dead, and you know how he feared the Lord. But now a creditor has come, threatening to take my two sons as slaves." "What can I do to help you?" Elisha asked. "Tell me, what do you have in the house?" "Nothing at all, except a flask of olive oil," she replied. And Elisha said, "Borrow as many empty jars as you can from your friends and neighbors. Then go into your house with your sons and shut the door behind you. Pour olive oil from your flask into the jars, setting each one aside when it is filled." *So she did as she was told.* Her sons kept bringing jars to her, and she filled one after another. Soon

every container was full to the brim! "Bring me another jar," she said to one of her sons. "There aren't any more!" he told her. And then the olive oil stopped flowing. When she told the man of God what had happened, he said to her, "Now sell the olive oil and pay your debts, and you and your sons can live on what is left over" (2 Kings 4:1–7, NLT; emphasis added).

Create or keep up your momentum by firmly plugging your faith into God through His word. By His grace, you too will receive the wisdom and strength that you need to find a solution or resolution to whatever you might be dealing with. After receiving God's instructions through His prophet, the widow took immediate *action*. The powerful weapons of God's word, accompanied with prayers and, when necessary, fasting—as God enables you to, and you are medically approved to do—will usually dislodge seemingly immovable situations in our lives. Because these spiritual protocols open our hearts and minds to receive God's clear instructions on how to move our situations forward. Put these truths into practice, and take whatever actions are needed. For "as the body apart from the spirit is dead, so also faith apart from works is dead" (James 2:26, ESV).

Are you willing to take the necessary actions as this poor widow did to move your own situation forward?

Chapter Twenty-One

HAVE A SNACK AND TAKE A NAP

The Prophet Elijah

The nation of Israel had fallen into idolatry by worshipping the false god, Baal. "Elijah the Tishbite, from Tishbe in Gilead, said to Ahab, 'As the Lord, the God of Israel, lives, whom I serve, there will be neither dew nor rain in the next few years except at my word'" (1 Kings 17:1, NIV). God honored the words of his servant, Prophet Elijah, and three years of a very severe famine followed. In the third year of the drought, Elijah decided to stage a major confrontation between himself—representing the one true God, Yahweh—and the false prophets of Baal—sponsored by King Ahab's wife, Jezebel. During the fierce encounter, all the false prophets were killed. The people repented and rededicated themselves to God, and Elijah prayed that God would send rain to the land (see 1 Kings 18). But when Queen Jezebel heard about all that Elijah had done, she was so furious that she threatened to kill him. This courageous prophet, who had just defeated their nation's false religious system, suddenly got so scared of this evil woman's threats that he fled into the wilderness. I think that Elijah had simply become so physically and emotionally exhausted after the intense spiritual battle that he just couldn't handle any more pressure. He fell into a deep state of fear and depression.

> When Ahab got home, he told Jezebel everything Elijah had done, including the way he had killed all the prophets of Baal. So Jezebel sent this message to Elijah: "May the gods strike me and even kill me if by this time tomorrow I have not killed you just as you killed them." Elijah was afraid and fled for his life. He went to Beersheba, a town in Judah, and he left his servant there. Then he went on alone into the wilderness, traveling all day. He sat down under a solitary broom tree and prayed that he might die. "I have had enough, Lord," he said. "Take my life, for I am no better than my ancestors who have already died." Then he lay down and slept under the broom tree. But as he was sleeping, an angel touched him and told him, *"Get up and eat!"* He looked around and there beside his head was some bread baked on hot stones and a jar of water! *So he ate and drank and lay down*

again. Then the angel of the Lord came again and touched him and said, *"Get up and eat some more, or the journey ahead will be too much for you." So he got up and ate and drank, and the food gave him enough strength to travel* forty days and forty nights to Mount Sinai, the mountain of God. There he came to a cave, where he spent the night (1 Kings 19:1–9, NLT).

So, here is our lesson from this great man of God's life:

Bodily fatigue and mental exhaustion can greatly contribute to a person's getting into a state of depression.

It is of vital importance to keep our physical bodies well-nourished with good food, while keeping our spirits and souls nourished with God's word. We must also prioritize being well rested as needed. While I am not at all suggesting that depression can always be remedied with simply a good meal and a restful nap. Because this was how God chose to handle Elijah's depression. Our loving creator gave food to human beings to nourish and reenergize their bodies.

> He makes grass grow for the cattle, and plants for people to cultivate—bringing forth food from the earth: and bread that sustains their hearts (Psalm 104:14–15, NIV).

Chapter Twenty-One

Jonathan

Another great example of the important role that eating nutritious meals regularly plays in our lives can be found in the story of Prince Jonathan. He was the son of King Saul, the first king of Israel.

> Now the men of Israel were pressed to exhaustion that day, because Saul had placed them under an oath, saying, "Let a curse fall on anyone who eats before evening—before I have full revenge on my enemies." So *no one ate anything all day,* even though they had all found honeycomb on the ground in the forest. They didn't dare touch the honey because they all feared the oath they had taken. But Jonathan had not heard his father's command, and he dipped the end of his stick into a piece of honeycomb and ate the honey. *After he had eaten it, he felt refreshed.* But one of the men saw him and said, *"Your father made the army take a strict oath that anyone who eats food today will be cursed. That is why everyone is weary and faint."* "My father has made trouble for us all!" Jonathan exclaimed. "A command like that only hurts us. See how refreshed I am now that I have eaten this little bit of honey. If the men had been allowed to eat freely from the food they found among our enemies, think how

many more Philistines we could have killed!" They chased and killed the Philistines all day from Micmash to Aijalon, growing more and more faint (I Samuel 14:24–31, NLT; emphasis added; see also I Samuel 28:22).

If the soldiers had simply been allowed to eat, they would have performed their jobs much better. But King Saul's unwise order almost brought their entire army's momentum to a grinding halt.

The Apostle Paul

We see this truth again in operation in the life of Apostle Paul, when the ship that he was traveling on suddenly was shipwrecked. Everyone on board rightly panicked, thinking that their lives were about to end. But Paul simply recommended that they should all eat first in order to replenish their energies and reignite momentum to battle the fierce storm. Just like Elijah, while battling the life-threatening storm, they had all lost their appetites and fallen into deep states of fear and depression.

> When a light wind began blowing from the south, the sailors thought they could make it. So they pulled up anchor and sailed close to

the shore of Crete. But the weather changed abruptly, and a wind of typhoon strength (called a "northeaster") burst across the island and blew us out to sea. The sailors couldn't turn the ship into the wind, so they gave up and let it run before the gale. We sailed along the sheltered side of a small island named Cauda, where with great difficulty we hoisted aboard the lifeboat being towed behind us. Then the sailors bound ropes around the hull of the ship to strengthen it. They were afraid of being driven across to the sandbars of Syrtis off the African coast, so they lowered the sea anchor to slow the ship and were driven before the wind. The next day, as gale-force winds continued to batter the ship, the crew began throwing the cargo overboard. The following day they even took some of the ship's gear and threw it overboard. The terrible storm raged for many days, blotting out the sun and the stars, until at last all hope was gone.

No one had eaten for a long time.

Finally, Paul called the crew together and said, "Men, you should have listened to me in the first place and not left Crete. You would have avoided all this damage and loss. But take courage! None of you will lose your lives, even though the ship will go down. For last night an angel of the God to whom I belong and whom

I serve stood beside me, and he said, 'Don't be afraid, Paul, for you will surely stand trial before Caesar! What's more, God in his goodness has granted safety to everyone sailing with you.' So take courage! For I believe God. It will be just as he said. But we will be shipwrecked on an island." About midnight on the fourteenth night of the storm, as we were being driven across the Sea of Adria, the sailors sensed land was near. They dropped a weighted line and found that the water was 120 feet deep. But a little later they measured again and found it was only 90 feet deep. At this rate they were afraid we would soon be driven against the rocks along the shore, so they threw out four anchors from the back of the ship and prayed for daylight. Then the sailors tried to abandon the ship; they lowered the lifeboat as though they were going to put out anchors from the front of the ship. But Paul said to the commanding officer and the soldiers, "You will all die unless the sailors stay aboard." So the soldiers cut the ropes to the lifeboat and let it drift away.

Just as day was dawning, Paul urged everyone to eat. "You have been so worried that you haven't touched food for two weeks," he said. "Please eat something now for your own good. For not a hair of your heads will perish." Then he took some bread, gave thanks to God before them all, and broke off a piece and ate it. Then everyone was encouraged and began to eat—all 276 of us who were on board.

After eating, the crew lightened the ship further by throwing the cargo of wheat overboard. When morning dawned, they didn't recognize the coastline, but they saw a bay with a beach and wondered if they could get to shore by running the ship aground. So they cut off the anchors and left them in the sea. Then they lowered the rudders, raised the foresail, and headed toward shore. But they hit a shoal and ran the ship aground too soon. The bow of the ship stuck fast, while the stern was repeatedly smashed by the force of the waves and began to break apart. The soldiers wanted to kill the prisoners to make sure they didn't swim ashore and escape. But the commanding officer wanted to spare Paul, so he didn't let them carry out their plan. Then he ordered all who could swim to jump overboard first and make for land. The others held on to planks or debris from the broken ship. So everyone escaped safely to shore (Acts 27:13–44, NLT; emphasis added)

A simple meal helped all the sailors to regain their momentum.

Paul had intentionally initiated this simple step of getting everyone to eat. Taking their minds off the problem and moving them forward. No one had eaten any food on the ship for several days. But Paul had faith in God that, just as He had promised, no one sailing on the ship with him would drown. After their meal, everyone made it safely to shore. Apostle Paul had used this practical method to reenergize everyone on board and give them hope. Remember that earlier on in our discussion, King David did the same thing to reenergize and move himself forward after mourning the death of his and Bathsheba's son.

> Then David got up from the ground. After he had washed, put on lotions and changed his clothes, he went into the house of the Lord and worshipped. Then he went to his own house, *and at his request they served him food, and he ate* (2 Samuel 12:20, NIV).

Maybe it's time for you to reignite your own momentum by taking a much-needed rest and nourishing your body with some nutritious food.

This might be a most simple method, but it is very effective. What do you think?

Chapter Twenty-Two

REIGNITING MOMENTUM AFTER A MAJOR STALEMATE

One of the definitions of stalemate is, "a situation in which further action or progress by opposing or competing parties seems impossible." This aptly captures the state of the relationship between two brothers who had become estranged due to a "cheating" incident. They were twins, and their names were Esau and Jacob. Esau was the firstborn and Jacob closely followed at the time of their birth. As the firstborn and eldest son of their father, Isaac, Esau was destined to inherit the covenant promise that God had first given to their grandfather, Abraham, which had been passed on to his first son who was their father, Isaac. This special blessing from God ensured that whoever received it would have a supernaturally blessed life. But Jacob, the younger brother, tricked his older brother, Esau, to snatch the irreplaceable blessing.

> One day when Jacob was cooking some stew, Esau arrived home from the wilderness exhausted and hungry. Esau said to Jacob, "I'm starved! Give

> me some of that red stew!" (This is how Esau got his other name, Edom, which means "red.") "All right," Jacob replied, "but trade me your rights as the firstborn son." "Look, I'm dying of starvation!" said Esau. "What good is my birthright to me now?" But Jacob said, "First you must swear that your birthright is mine." So, Esau swore an oath, thereby selling all his rights as the firstborn to his brother, Jacob. Then Jacob gave Esau some bread and lentil stew. Esau ate the meal, then got up and left. He showed contempt for his rights as the firstborn. (Genesis 25:29–34, NLT).

Sometime after the preceding event took place, this happened:

> One day when Isaac was old and turning blind, he called for Esau, his older son, and said, "My son." "Yes, Father?" Esau replied. "I am an old man now," Isaac said, "and I don't know when I may die. Take your bow and a quiver full of arrows, and go out into the open country to hunt some wild game for me. Prepare my favorite dish, and bring it here for me to eat. Then I will pronounce the blessing that belongs to you, my firstborn son, before I die." But Rebekah overheard what Isaac had said to his son Esau.

So when Esau left to hunt for the wild game, she said to her son Jacob, "Listen. I overheard your father say to Esau, 'Bring me some wild game and prepare me a delicious meal. Then I will bless you in the Lord's presence before I die.' Now, my son, listen to me. Do exactly as I tell you. Go out to the flocks, and bring me two fine young goats. I'll use them to prepare your father's favorite dish. Then take the food to your father so he can eat it and bless you before he dies." "But look," Jacob replied to Rebekah, "my brother, Esau, is a hairy man, and my skin is smooth. What if my father touches me? He'll see that I'm trying to trick him, and then he'll curse me instead of blessing me."

But his mother replied, "Then let the curse fall on me, my son! Just do what I tell you. Go out and get the goats for me!" So Jacob went out and got the young goats for his mother. Rebekah took them and prepared a delicious meal, just the way Isaac liked it. Then she took Esau's favorite clothes, which were there in the house, and gave them to her younger son, Jacob. She covered his arms and the smooth part of his neck with the skin of the young goats. Then she gave Jacob the delicious meal, including freshly baked bread. So Jacob took the food to his father. "My father?" he said. "Yes, my son," Isaac answered. "Who are you—Esau or Jacob?" Jacob replied, "It's Esau, your firstborn son. I've done as you told me. Here is the wild game. Now sit up and eat it so you can give me your blessing." Isaac asked, "How did you find it so quickly, my son?" "The Lord your God put it in my path!" Jacob replied.

Then Isaac said to Jacob, "Come closer so I can touch you and make sure that you really are Esau." So Jacob went closer to his father, and Isaac touched him. "The voice is Jacob's, but the hands are Esau's," Isaac said. But he did not recognize Jacob, because Jacob's hands felt hairy just like Esau's. So Isaac prepared to bless Jacob. "But are you really my son Esau?" he asked. "Yes, I am," Jacob replied. Then Isaac said, "Now, my son, bring me the wild game. Let me eat it, and then I will give you my blessing." So Jacob took the food to his father, and Isaac ate it. He also drank the wine that Jacob served him. Then Isaac said to Jacob, "Please come a little closer and kiss me, my son." So Jacob went over and kissed him. And when Isaac caught the smell of his clothes, he was finally convinced, and he blessed his son (Genesis 27:1–27, NLT).

From that time on, Esau hated Jacob because their father had given Jacob the blessing. And Esau began to scheme: "I will soon be mourning my father's death. Then I will kill my brother, Jacob." But Rebekah heard about Esau's plans. So she sent for Jacob and told him, "Listen, Esau is consoling himself by plotting to kill you. So listen carefully, my son. Get ready and flee to my brother, Laban, in Haran. Stay there with him until your brother cools off. When he calms down and forgets what you have done to him, I will send for you to come back. Why should I lose both of you in one day?" (Genesis 27:41–45, NLT).

As we just read, Jacob who had been prompted by their mother, Rebekah, impersonated and stole the blessing from his older brother, Esau. Do you think that Jacob was wrong in attempting to collect on the earlier transaction that he had made with older brother Esau? While I do not at all absolve Jacob from his adult responsibility of saying no to the ungodly and devious advice given to him by his mother, he must have thought that he was entitled to this blessing, based on Esau's foolish sale of his birthright.

This was an ungodly method to try to bring about what someone believed was God's will. But lying and stealing will never be the right way to receive God's blessings.

To better understand Rebekah's motive for advising her younger son to cheat her elder son in this way, we must take a quick look at an incident that took place while Rebekah was pregnant with her twins. It might help us to understand her a bit. Based on that incident, she probably thought that she was obeying God when she made this extremely poor choice that would create a lifelong stalemate between her beloved sons.

> Isaac pleaded with the Lord on behalf of his wife, because she was unable to have children. The Lord answered Isaac's prayer, and Rebekah became pregnant with twins. But the two children struggled with each other in her womb. So she went to ask the Lord about it. "Why is this happening to me?" she asked. And the Lord told her, "The sons in your womb will become two nations. From the very beginning, the two nations will be rivals. One nation will be stronger than the other; and your older son will serve your younger son." And when the time came to give birth, Rebekah discovered that she did indeed have twins! The first one was very red at birth and covered with thick hair like a fur coat. So, they named him Esau. Then the other twin was

born with his hand grasping Esau's heel. So, they named him Jacob (Genesis 25:21–26, NLT).

Nevertheless, Rebekah was wrong. Her deceitful counsel to her younger and favorite son, Jacob, irreversibly damaged their family (see also Genesis 25:28). Here is an important lesson:

Parents must firmly resist the temptation to play favorites among their children. This is a big no-no. It creates jealousy and division among them that can destroy the family.

This incident almost led to the two men killing each other, and it was completely unnecessary to do things in this way. God can take care of fulfilling His own promises. We don't have to cheat, disobey Him, or ever take matters into our own hands in the way that Rebekah did. Using ungodly methods to try to accomplish God's plans and purposes will only create havoc.

Both the processes that we use and the end results that we seek must be righteously achieved.

Jacob had to flee from Esau to avoid getting killed, but many years later, the situation could no longer be avoided. Because Jacob wanted to return home from his self-imposed exile. So, he had to take ownership of his past sins, and the primary responsibility for this major stalemate. Jacob initiated the reconciliation process in order to ignite momentum and move his relationship with Esau forward in a positive direction. His efforts to return home would require divine help, because rightly or wrongly, Esau now detested his twin brother.

> *How on earth do we appease someone who loathes us, when every memory of us causes them pain?*

Well, Jacob is about to teach all of us this important lesson. And as I have said many times in our discussion, we first seek God's help. He is the only one who can touch and change human hearts, softening them to grant us favor with whomever we're seeking to meet or reconcile with. "In the LORD's hand the king's heart is a stream of water that he channels toward all who please him" (Proverbs 21:1, NIV).

Then they celebrated the Festival of Unleavened Bread for seven days. There was great joy throughout the land *because the LORD had caused the king of Assyria to be favorable to them,* so that he helped them to rebuild the Temple of God, the God of Israel (Ezra 6:22, NLT; emphasis added).

> Then Jacob prayed, "O God of my grandfather Abraham, and God of my father, Isaac—O Lord, you told me, 'Return to your own land

and to your relatives.' And you promised me, 'I will treat you kindly.' I am not worthy of all the unfailing love and faithfulness you have shown to me, your servant. When I left home and crossed the Jordan River, I owned nothing except a walking stick. Now my household fills two large camps! O Lord, please rescue me from the hand of my brother, Esau. I am afraid that he is coming to attack me, along with my wives and children. But you promised me, 'I will surely treat you kindly, and I will multiply your descendants until they become as numerous as the sands along the seashore—too many to count'" (Genesis 32:9–12, NLT).

After seeking God for help—and this is my personal favorite Jacob move—Jacob got Esau lots and lots and lots of gifts! Simple right? (Chuckle). But no kidding, Jacob had received wisdom from God and went about things right this time. This was a very wise move, because we all love to receive gifts.

> A gift given in secret soothes anger (Proverbs 21:14, NIV).

> Giving a gift can open doors; it gives access to important people! (Proverbs 18:16, NLT).

Many seek favors from a ruler; everyone is the friend of a person who gives gifts! (Proverbs 19:6, NLT).

Jacob stayed where he was for the night. Then he selected these gifts from his possessions to present to his brother, Esau: 200 female goats, 20 male goats, 200 ewes, 20 rams, 30 female camels with their young, 40 cows, 10 bulls, 20 female donkeys, and 10 male donkeys. He divided these animals into herds and assigned each to different servants. Then he told his servants, "Go ahead of me with the animals, but keep some distance between the herds." He gave these instructions to the men leading the first group: "When my brother, Esau, meets you, he will ask, 'whose servants are you? Where are you going? Who owns these animals?' You must reply, 'They belong to your servant Jacob, but they are a gift for his master Esau. Look, he is coming right behind us.'" Jacob gave the same instructions to the second and third herdsmen and to all who followed behind the herds: "You must say the same thing to Esau when you meet him. And be sure to say, 'Look, your servant Jacob is right behind us.'" Jacob thought, *"I will try to appease him by sending gifts ahead of me.* When I see him in person, perhaps he will be friendly to me." So the gifts were sent on ahead, while Jacob himself spent that night in the camp (Genesis 32:13–21, NLT; emphasis added).

Jacob did the preceding in order to find favor with Esau, and put an end to the long stalemate between them. After doing all these things, he then went to meet Esau. Another takeaway,

> *We all need to be willing to humble ourselves and take responsibility for any actions on our part that may have created or contributed to a state of stalemate.*

"Then Jacob went on ahead. As he approached his brother, he bowed to the ground seven times before him. Then Esau ran to meet him and embraced him, threw his arms around his neck, and kissed him. And they both wept" (Genesis 33:3–4, NLT). Seeking forgiveness from those whom we may have hurt by our wrong actions is an unavoidable part of genuinely repenting and reigniting momentum after a stalemate. Alexander Pope, an English poet, said the following:

> *"A man should never be ashamed to own he has been in the wrong, which is but saying, in other words, that he is wiser today than he was yesterday."*

The rift between the two brothers came to an end after so many years, when one of them took the initiative to create momentum and restore harmony between them. With God's help, this led to a joyful reconciliation. So, let's all be courageous, seek God for His help, and humbly do all that is within our power to be the peacemaker who brings reconciliation to our families, communities, and nation. I know that this will not always be easy to accomplish, but if we desire to end any stalemate situations in our own lives, this is what it will take.

Are we willing to swallow our pride, let go of all self-justification, and genuinely ask for forgiveness from anyone whom we might have hurt or offended?

Chapter Twenty-Three

How to Defeat Haters

I have reiterated throughout our discussion that, in order to keep up our momentum and experience nonstop progress in our lives, we must practice good spiritual habits on a daily basis. This is indispensable to a successful lifestyle. Making spiritual wellness a priority will serve us well in both the good and the bad times. God's word is the truth upon which we can securely and successfully build our lives. He has promised to empower us with His grace to overcome life's most difficult trials and adversities. Reading and meditating on God's word, seeking Him daily through our prayers, and reflecting on how our own choices shape our lives, will help us to stay connected to the source of our lives and strength: God.

Another great example of how faith can greatly impact our ability to ignite or keep up our momentum is from one of my favorite people in the Bible, Governor Daniel. I talked about him in a previous discussion in my book *All Will Be Well: Receiving the Keys to Strengthen Your Faith*, but he is also relevant to our current theme. His life holds so many valuable lessons for us. Daniel shows us through his lifestyle that staying connected to God is how we can stay strong and overcome the fiercest adversarial attacks. He was one of the King of Babylon's top three advisers and was just about to be promoted again to become second in charge only to the King when some very powerful people in the country came against him. Because of their envy, they were determined to put an end to Daniel's momentum. Their hatred might also have been connected to the fact that Daniel was not a Babylonian by birth, but still got to hold their country's topmost powerful positions. Daniel was from the tribe of Judah in Israel, and he had been forcefully taken to Babylon as a slave in his teenage years, when the nation of Israel lost a brutal war to the Babylonians.

> Darius the Mede decided to divide the kingdom into 120 provinces, and he appointed a high officer to rule over each province. The king also chose Daniel and two others as administrators to supervise the high officers and protect the king's interests. Daniel soon proved himself more capable than all the other administrators and high officers. Because of Daniel's great ability, the king made plans to place him over the entire empire. Then the other administrators and high officers began searching for some fault in the way Daniel was handling government affairs, but they couldn't find anything

to criticize or condemn. He was faithful, always responsible, and completely trustworthy. So they concluded, "Our only chance of finding grounds for accusing Daniel will be in connection with the rules of his religion."

So the administrators and high officers went to the king and said, "Long live King Darius! We are all in agreement—we administrators, officials, high officers, advisers, and governors—that the king should make a law that will be strictly enforced. Give orders that for the next thirty days any person who prays to anyone, divine or human—except to you, Your Majesty—will be thrown into the den of lions. And now, Your Majesty, issue and sign this law so it cannot be changed, an official law of the Medes and Persians that cannot be revoked." So, King Darius signed the law.

But when Daniel learned that the law had been signed, he went home and knelt down as usual in his upstairs room, with its windows open toward Jerusalem. He prayed three times a day, just as he had always done, giving thanks to his God (Daniel 6:1–10, NLT).

Daniel's instant response to this vicious attack was to simply continue praying three times a day, just as he had always done. He knew that his life was ultimately in

God's hands and not in the hands of the Babylonians. So, he continued to practice the good spiritual habits that he had done before this fierce attack.

> *Our daily spiritual routines are of the utmost importance. They will determine how we respond if we're suddenly confronted with any unexpected challenges.*

Building our lives on the solid rock of obedience to God's word will provide us with the support that we need in all circumstances.

> So why do you keep calling me "Lord, Lord!" when you don't do what I say? I will show you what it's like when someone comes to me, listens to my teaching, and then follows it. It is like a person building a house who digs deep and lays the foundation on solid rock. When the floodwaters rise and break against that house, it stands firm because it is well built. But anyone who hears and doesn't obey is like a person who builds a house right on the ground, without a foundation. When the floods sweep down against that house, it will collapse into a heap of ruins (Luke 6:46–49, NLT).

The sort of rapid and unperturbed reaction that Daniel displayed to such a ferocious attack against him can only happen when a person has been strengthening their faith muscles daily. Although he had been forced into slavery as a lad, Daniel kept his mind and heart free from captivity by staying closely connected to the God of Israel. He kept his faith strong while living in Babylon, and this was the reason why he refused to pray to any human being as the King had ordered. This sounds similar to the attitude that another Jewish man, Mordecai, had when he was asked to bow to an official while living in Persia. Daniel was also a man who practiced what he believed. So, here is another important lesson from this devoted man's life:

> *Never discard your faith in God or your righteous principles, even if you're living or doing business in hostile environments.*

Daniel's example demonstrates to all of us that we can still maintain our faith in God even while in an environment that opposes our beliefs. If we find ourselves living in or doing business in an ungodly environment, we mustn't allow ourselves to be deterred or intimidated by this. Daniel kept his mind free and fixed on Jerusalem in Judah. He had always prayed three times a day before the attack, so with his windows wide open toward Jerusalem, Daniel simply did what he had always done to keep up his spiritual momentum daily. Jerusalem had been considered to be the capital of the kingdom of Judah at that time. Judah means praise. So, this is a good reminder:

> *A lifestyle of giving praises, thanks, and worship*
> *to God is vital to staying spiritually strong.*

This is the way that we can *express* our love to God for all that he has done for us. Daniel did not let his location or slave status alter his devotion to God. "If I forget you, Jerusalem, may my right hand forget its skill. May my tongue cling to the roof of my mouth if I do not remember you, if I do not consider Jerusalem my highest joy" (Psalm 137:5–6, NIV).

> *If you were suddenly blindsided by an unexpected*
> *challenge as Daniel was, would you be too scared*
> *to know what to do, or would you be able to rely*
> *on your daily spiritual practices, as he did?*

Stay closely connected to your source of strength, and rely daily on God's grace within you to stay strong in all circumstances.

> "Can an Ethiopian change his skin or a leopard its spots? Neither can you do good who are accustomed to doing evil" (Jeremiah 13:23, NIV).

In other words, the things that we do regularly will play a big role in shaping our destinies. For example, if we're accustomed to living defiantly or rebelliously toward God, these sorts of habits will not support or serve us well during challenging times. Daniel would eventually prevail over his enemies because he had built his life on the solid rock of obedience to God's word.

> "The earnest prayer of a righteous person has great power and produces wonderful results" (James 5:16, NLT).

Here is how this life-threatening episode in this devoted man's life came to a conclusion:

> Then the officials went together to Daniel's house and found him praying and asking for God's help. So they went straight to the king and and reminded him about his law. "Did you not sign a law that for the next thirty days any person who prays to anyone, divine or human—except to you, Your Majesty—will be thrown into the den of lions?" "Yes," the king replied, "that decision stands; it is an official law of the Medes and Persians that cannot be revoked." Then they told the king, "That man Daniel, one of the captives from Judah, is ignoring you and your law. He still prays to his God three times a day." Hearing this, the king was deeply troubled, and he tried to think of a way to save

Daniel. He spent the rest of the day looking for a way to get Daniel out of this predicament. In the evening the men went together to the king and said, "Your Majesty, you know that according to the law of the Medes and the Persians, no law that the king signs can be changed."

So at last the king gave orders for Daniel to be arrested and thrown into the den of lions. The king said to him, "May your God, whom you serve so faithfully, rescue you." A stone was brought and placed over the mouth of the den. The king sealed the stone with his own royal seal and the seals of his nobles, so that no one could rescue Daniel. Then the king returned to his palace and spent the night fasting. He refused his usual entertainment and couldn't sleep at all that night. Very early the next morning, the king got up and hurried out to the lions' den. When he got there, he called out in anguish, "Daniel, servant of the living God! Was your God, whom you serve so faithfully, able to rescue you from the lions?" Daniel answered, "Long live the king! My God sent his angel to shut the lions' mouths so that they would not hurt me, for I have been found innocent in his sight. And I have not wronged you, Your Majesty."

The king was overjoyed and ordered that Daniel be lifted from the den. Not a scratch was found on him, for he had trusted in his God. Then the king gave orders to arrest the men who had maliciously accused Daniel. He had them thrown into the lions' den, along with their wives and children. The lions leaped on them and tore them apart before they even hit the floor of the den. Then King Darius sent this message to the people of every race and nation and language throughout the world: "Peace and prosperity to you! I decree that everyone throughout my kingdom should tremble with fear before the God of Daniel. For he is the living God, and he will endure forever. His kingdom will never be destroyed, and his rule will never end. He rescues and saves his people; he performs miraculous signs and wonders in the heavens and on earth. He has rescued Daniel from the power of the lions." So Daniel prospered during the reign of Darius and the reign of Cyrus the Persian (Daniel 6:11–28, NLT).

God protected and granted Daniel favor with the king of Babylon, and he triumphed mightily over his vicious enemies. Daniel would go on to serve four more kings who ruled over the great empire. "The lovers of God who chase after righteousness will find all their dreams come true: an abundant life drenched with favor and a fountain that overflows with satisfaction" (Proverbs 21:21, The Passion Translation).

> So, "Be strong and courageous! Do not be afraid and do not panic before them. For the LORD your God will personally go ahead of you. He will neither fail you nor abandon you" (Deuteronomy 31:6, NLT).

Whenever we feel as if we're all out of options and want to give up, let us choose to believe in God and *proceed*. Having faith in Him is the most powerful weapon in our arsenal. No matter how long you've been stuck in your current situation, make the decision today to move forward.

> For we are His workmanship [His own master work, a work of art], created in Christ Jesus [reborn from above—spiritually transformed, renewed, ready to be used] for good works, which God prepared [for us] beforehand [taking paths which He set], so that we would walk in them [living the good life which He prearranged and made ready for us] (Ephesians 2:10, AMP; brackets in the original).

While the miraculous things that God chooses to do in our own lives may not always be quite as spectacular as some of the ones that we've read, simply receiving the strength from Him to go on is a huge miracle in itself, especially when we're at our lowest. Apply this powerful key of unleashing momentum to your life on a consistent basis, and your life and the lives of others around you will be positively impacted. Spend time daily in God's presence. This will release His grace into your life to triumph as Governor Daniel did.

Are you losing or keeping up your momentum based on your present daily spiritual habits?

Chapter Twenty-Four

God's Powerful Example

We cannot end our discussion without including the powerful example set by God after the fall of the first two human beings that He had created, Adam and Eve (see Genesis, 1–3). They were the original parents of all human beings, and the masterpiece of God's creation. These two lived in the beautiful Garden of Eden that God had planted with His own hands for them. Moving around freely on the amazing planet that He had magnanimously gifted to them. All that was expected of Adam and Eve was that they obey God's commands, and be good stewards of their new planet.

God was their great benefactor, and the source of their lives and all their blessings. He was also the only one with the perfect understanding of how everything that He had created, including human beings, worked. So, following His commands was vital to their survival and prosperity. Their creator also gave Adam and Eve complete dominion over their planet. But after they had received all these immense blessings from God, instead of loving Him back, Adam and Eve responded to His enormous magnanimity with incomprehensible distrust. The enemy of all that was good had sneaked into their garden and successfully tempted the first two human beings to fall away completely from God.

> Now the serpent was more crafty than any beast of the field which the Lord God had made. And he said to the woman, "Indeed, has God said, you shall not eat from any tree of the garden?" The woman said to the serpent, "From the fruit of the trees of the garden we may eat; but from the fruit of the tree which is in the middle of the garden, God has said, 'You shall not eat from it or touch it, or you will die.'" The serpent said to the woman, "You surely will not die! For God knows that in the day you eat from it your eyes will be opened, and you will be like God, knowing good and evil."
>
> When the woman saw that the tree was good for food, and that it was a delight to the eyes, and that the tree was desirable to make one wise, she took from its fruit and ate; and she gave also to her husband with her, and he ate. Then the eyes of both of them were opened, and they knew that they were naked; and they sewed fig leaves together and made themselves loin coverings. They heard the sound of the LORD God walking in the garden in the cool of the day, and the man and his wife hid themselves from the presence of the LORD

God among the trees of the garden. Then the LORD God called to the man, and said to him, "Where are you?" He said, "I heard the sound of You in the garden, and I was afraid because I was naked; so I hid myself." And He said, "Who told you that you were naked? Have you eaten from the tree of which I commanded you not to eat?" (Genesis 3:1–11, NASB 1995).

God's dream of having human beings in His family appeared to be irreversibly shattered. His response to Adam and Eve's treachery had to be swift and drastic. His judgment and punishment were promptly issued in comparable levels to the revelation of His person that they had both been privileged to have. Everyone involved in the great fiasco had to take responsibility for their own individual contribution.

> Then the Lord God said to the serpent, "Because you have done this, you are cursed more than all animals, domestic and wild. You will crawl on your belly, groveling in the dust as long as you live. And I will cause hostility between you and the woman, and between your offspring and her offspring. He will strike your head, and you will strike his heel." Then he said to the woman, "I will sharpen the pain of your pregnancy, and in pain you will give birth. And you will desire to control

your husband, but he will rule over you." And to the man he said, "Since you listened to your wife and ate from the tree whose fruit I commanded you not to eat, the ground is cursed because of you. All your life you will struggle to scratch a living from it. It will grow thorns and thistles for you, though you will eat of its grains. By the sweat of your brow will you have food to eat until you return to the ground from which you were made. For you were made from dust, and to dust you will return" (Genesis 3:14–19, NASB).

Therefore the Lord God sent him out from the Garden of Eden, to cultivate the ground from which he was taken. He drove the man out; and at the east of the Garden of Eden he stationed the cherubim and the flaming sword which turned every direction to guard the way to the tree of life (Genesis 3:23–24, ESV).

Spiritually, physically, morally, and in every other way, Adam and Eve were completely broken. They had to leave their beautiful garden behind to restart life without God in the dark unknown. This must have been one of the saddest days for our Creator. The day He seemingly lost His human family forever. The only day that would far surpass this one in the level of pain that God would have to endure was when He had to offer up His only begotten Son to redeem human beings from their devastating fall. After punishing all the participants in the gigantic mess,

> *God reignited momentum and began to make a new way for the masterpiece of His creation, human beings, to be restored back into His family.*

As far as our loving creator was concerned, any attack against His children was an attack against Him. The many steps that God would implement to make it possible for human beings to be restored into His family would ultimately culminate in the death of His only begotten Son, Jesus Christ, on the cross for humankind's sins.

> "For God so [greatly] loved and dearly prized the world, that He [even] gave His [One and] only begotten Son, so that whoever believes and trusts in Him [as Savior] shall not perish, but have eternal life" (John 3:16, AMP; brackets in the original).

> Even before he made the world, God loved us and chose us in Christ to be holy and without fault in his eyes. God decided in advance to adopt us into his own family by bringing us to himself through Jesus Christ (Ephesians 1:4–5, NLT).

> The Lamb who was slain from the creation of the world (Revelation 13:8, NIV).

In the midst of the most awful devastation, God did not give up on human beings but, instead, proceeded to give all of creation the greatest lesson on love and reigniting momentum ever known.

Because God loved human beings so much, He was not going to ever give up on having us in His family. He did not at all take things lying down. In order to rescue them, our loving creator would ultimately destroy the forces of evil that took His children captive, taking upon Himself the full responsibility for human being's sin against Him. His loving response far surpassed anything that anyone could ever have imagined. He promptly offered Adam and Eve forgiveness, because the stated punishment for their sins was death.

> But you must not eat from the tree of the knowledge of good and evil, for when you eat from it you will certainly die (Genesis 2:17, NIV).

> For the wages of sin is death, but the free gift of God is eternal life through Christ Jesus our Lord (Romans 6:23, NLT).

God substituted the blood of sinless, innocent animals for their sins, preventing their instant and eternal demises. This was the only way that He could temporarily cover their sins, until the time when the perfect sacrifice of His only begotten son, Jesus Christ could fully pay for and take away all humankind's sins. "And the Lord God made clothing from animal skins for Adam and his wife" (Genesis 3:21, NIV). God had shown the depths of His amazing grace and mercy by not destroying the first two human beings and relegating them to the scrap heap. This would have been by far the simplest and least painful option for our creator to take. He could have destroyed Adam and Eve before they started to multiply and made an entirely new type of creature for Himself. But all praises be to God! After ultimate evil had successfully attacked God's dream of having human beings in His family forever, the scriptures tell us that God showed us His loving kindness. God continued the enormous task of rescuing human beings and restoring His entire creation when He pushed back fiercely against this catastrophic series of events.

He would not give up on us. Instead,
God reignited His momentum.

Our creator's unfathomable love for us is way beyond our comprehension. So, it behooves us to swiftly take full advantage of the free pardon that God offers all human beings through the sacrifice of His only begotten son,

Jesus Christ, on the cross for our sins. Unlike Adam and Eve, our original parents, who responded to God's love and generosity with distrust and betrayal, the only fitting response on our part is to show our love and gratitude toward our creator. Because,

> When we were utterly helpless, Christ came at just the right time and died for us sinners. Now, most people would not be willing to die for an upright person, though someone might perhaps be willing to die for a person who is especially good. But God showed his great love for us by sending Christ to die for us while we were still sinners. And since we have been made right in God's sight by the blood of Christ, he will certainly save us from God's condemnation. For since our friendship with God was restored by the death of his Son while we were still his enemies, we will certainly be saved through the life of his Son. So now we can rejoice in our wonderful new relationship with God because our Lord Jesus Christ has made us friends of God. When Adam sinned, sin entered the world. Adam's sin brought death, so death spread to everyone, for everyone sinned.... But there is a great difference between Adam's sin and God's gracious gift. For the sin of this one man, Adam, brought death to many. But even greater is God's

wonderful grace and his gift of forgiveness to many through this other man, Jesus Christ. And the result of God's gracious gift is very different from the result of that one man's sin. For Adam's sin led to condemnation, but God's free gift leads to our being made right with God, even though we are guilty of many sins. For the sin of this one man, Adam, caused death to rule over many. But even greater is God's wonderful grace and his gift of righteousness, for all who receive it will live in triumph over sin and death through this one man, Jesus Christ. Yes, Adam's one sin brings condemnation for everyone, but Christ's one act of righteousness brings a right relationship with God and new life for everyone (Romans 5:6–12, 15–18, NLT).

God reignited His momentum and moved things forward after the fall of human beings. Will you choose to move things forward positively in your own life if you have experienced a major failure?

The preceding chapter, "God's Powerful Example," included modified excerpts from my book *Giving God Ultimate Love, Over-the-Top Mega Love* relating to the immediate steps that God took to recover His lost family and creation after human beings' fall.

Chapter Twenty-Five

RUTH: THE QUEEN OF MOMENTUM

I would like to wrap up our discussion with a final example from the life of a fine young woman by the name of Ruth. She was a Moabite by birth, and after life had dealt her some very heavy blows, she revealed her loyal and courageous nature through her actions.

> In the days when the judges ruled, there was a famine in the land. So a man from Bethlehem in Judah, together with his wife and two sons, went to live for a while in the country of Moab. The man's name was Elimelek, his wife's name was Naomi, and the names of his two sons were Mahlon and Kilion. They were Ephrathites from Bethlehem, Judah. And they went to Moab and lived there. Now Elimelek, Naomi's husband, died, and she was left with her two sons. They married Moabite women, one named Orpah and the other Ruth. After they had lived there about ten years, both Mahlon and Kilion also died, and Naomi was left without her two

sons and her husband. When Naomi heard in Moab that the Lord had come to the aid of his people by providing food for them, she and her daughters-in-law prepared to return home from there. With her two daughters-in-law she left the place where she had been living and set out on the road that would take them back to the land of Judah.

Then Naomi said to her two daughters-in-law, "Go back, each of you, to your mother's home. May the Lord show you kindness, as you have shown kindness to your dead husbands and to me. May the Lord grant that each of you will find rest in the home of another husband." Then she kissed them goodbye and they wept aloud and said to her, "We will go back with you to your people." But Naomi said, "Return home, my daughters. Why would you come with me? Am I going to have any more sons, who could become your husbands? Return home, my daughters; I am too old to have another husband. Even if I thought there was still hope for me—even if I had a husband tonight and then gave birth to sons—would you wait until they grew up? Would you remain unmarried for them? No, my daughters. It is more bitter for me than for you, because the Lord's hand has turned against me!" At this they wept aloud again. Then Orpah kissed her mother-in-law goodbye, but Ruth clung to her. "Look," said Naomi, "your sister-in-law is going back to her people and her gods. Go back with her."

But Ruth replied, "Don't urge me to leave you or to turn back from you. Where you go I will go, and where you stay I will stay. Your people will be my people and your God my God. Where you die I will die, and there I will be buried. May the Lord deal with me, be it ever so severely, if even death separates you and me."

When Naomi realized that Ruth was determined to go with her, she stopped urging her. So the two women went on until they came to Bethlehem. When they arrived in Bethlehem, the whole town was stirred because of them, and the women exclaimed, "Can this be Naomi?" "Don't call me Naomi," she told them. "Call me Mara, because the Almighty has made my life very bitter. I went away full, but the Lord has brought me back empty. Why call me Naomi? The Lord has afflicted me; the Almighty has brought misfortune upon me." So Naomi returned from Moab accompanied by Ruth the Moabite, her daughter-in-law, arriving in Bethlehem as the barley harvest was beginning (Ruth 1, NIV; emphasis added).

After their family had suffered a horrendous string of losses, instead of staying stuck and getting bitter, Ruth revealed the depth of her virtuous character. She was still a young and attractive woman, so she could have stayed in Moab and remarried in her homeland, which was familiar territory. But this amazing young woman proved her devotion to God and her family by recommitting herself afresh to Naomi and moving forward.

After suffering from a major loss or failure, moving forward in whatever positive ways that we still can, will open the door for new blessings from God to flow into our own lives, and through us to others.

After experiencing famine and the loss of their loved ones, both Naomi and Ruth must have been very tempted to give up on their lives. Doubting whether the God of Israel was truly the one to follow if things could go so horribly wrong. But instead, they unequivocally committed themselves to the God of Israel. Sometime after their arrival back in Israel, Naomi began to make fresh plans for her devoted daughter-in-law to be remarried. So, she carefully guided her into a successful union with a close relative of theirs by the name of Boaz. He was the one who was in line to help Naomi reclaim all her family's property that had been left behind when they immigrated to Moab. Through the favor and special hand of God upon Ruth, she became Boaz's wife.

> Then Boaz said to the elders and to the crowd standing around, "You are witnesses that today I have bought from Naomi all the property of Elimelech, Kilion, and Mahlon. And with the land I have acquired Ruth, the Moabite widow of Mahlon, to be my wife. This way she can have a son to carry on the family name of her dead husband and to inherit the family property here in his hometown. You are all witnesses today." Then the elders and all the people standing in the gate replied, "We are witnesses! May the Lord make this woman who is coming into your home like Rachel and Leah, from whom all the nation of Israel descended! May you prosper in Ephrathah and be famous in Bethlehem. And may the Lord give you descendants by this young woman who will be like those of our ancestor Perez, the son of Tamar and Judah."
>
> *So, Boaz took Ruth into his home, and she became his wife.* When he slept with her, the Lord enabled her to become pregnant, and she gave birth to a son. Then the women of the town said to Naomi, "Praise the Lord, who has now provided a redeemer for your family! May this child be famous in Israel. May he restore your youth

and care for you in your old age. For he is the son of your daughter-in-law who loves you and has been better to you than seven sons!" Naomi took the baby and cuddled him to her breast. And she cared for him as if he were her own. The neighbor women said, "Now at last Naomi has a son again!" And they named him Obed. He became the father of Jesse and the grandfather of David (Ruth 4:9–17, NLT; emphasis added).

Ruth's outstanding legacy of devotion to God and her family was richly rewarded by God. She went on to be listed in the lineage of God's only begotten son, Jesus Christ, the Savior of the world, through King David of Israel's family line.

This is a record of the ancestors of Jesus the Messiah, a descendant of David and of Abraham. Abraham was the father of Isaac. Isaac was the father of Jacob. Jacob was the father of Judah and his brothers. Judah was the father of Perez and Zerah (whose mother was Tamar). Perez was the father of Hezron. Hezron was the father of Ram. Ram was the father of Amminadab. Amminadab was the father of Nahshon. Nahshon was the father of Salmon. Salmon was the father of Boaz (whose mother was Rahab). *Boaz was the father of Obed (whose mother was Ruth). Obed was the*

father of Jesse. Jesse was the father of King David.
David was the father of Solomon (whose mother was Bathsheba, the widow of Uriah) (Matthew 1:1–6, NLT; emphasis added).

After having failed in her first attempt to raise a successful family, Naomi was strengthened by her loving and devoted daughter-in-law to recover all that she had lost. These two women could easily have given up on their faith in God, but they were greatly favored by Him when they returned to Israel. Ruth became the wife of an extremely wealthy man, and successfully raised a renowned family. "To all who mourn in Israel, he will give a crown of beauty for ashes, a joyous blessing instead of mourning, festive praise instead of despair. In their righteousness, they will be like great oaks that the LORD has planted for his own glory" (Isaiah 61:3, NLT).

> For the LORD takes pleasure in His people; He adorns the afflicted with salvation (Psalm 149:4, BSB).

Will you start to consistently unleash the powerful principle of momentum in your own life to propel yourself forward toward nonstop progress and success?

Are you willing to open your heart to the possibility of starting over after experiencing

*a great loss as this young woman and
her mother-in-law, Naomi, did?*

I pray that this discussion will help you to recommit to unleashing this powerful key to success—*momentum*—in your own life.

God bless you!

Bukky Agboola

OTHER BOOKS BY BUKKY AGBOOLA

Giving God Ultimate Love

All Will Be Well

I Made it Through

www.ingramcontent.com/pod-product-compliance
Lightning Source LLC
Chambersburg PA
CBHW030545080526
44585CB00012B/264